STOP

READING

WORD

BY

WORD!

Do you read a single word at a time?
Do you miss key words and have to re-read?
Do you move your lips when you read silently?
Do you hear the words in your head as you
   read?
Do you have difficulty grasping material you
   have to read quickly?

Whether your reading is handicapped by these habits or whether it's simply a matter of too much to read and too little time, this remarkable guidebook will show you how to read with CONFIDENCE, SPEED AND COMPRE-HENSION.

The miraculous new methods offered in these pages have been scientifically tested and developed by experts. They are simple to understand and easy to follow.

Let this book be your key to an exciting new world of knowledge and enjoyment.

READ FOR PLEASURE—READ FOR PROFIT.

DOUBLE YOUR READING SPEED

DOUBLE
Your Reading
Speed

by THE READING LABORATORY, Inc.

FAWCETT PREMIER • NEW YORK

Contents

PART TWO

DAY I

DAY II

DAY III

DAY IV

DAY X

DOUBLE
Your Reading
Speed

One Million Words!

A huge number of words! Yet it has been estimated that a college student or an average man in a position of average responsibility may be expected to read up to, and in many cases even more than, one million words *in a single week!* Can *you* handle that?

Before you read any further, get a watch with a sweep second hand and begin timing yourself through the rest of this section—START—to see how your reading abilities stack up against the reading load you now have to handle. Think of the flood of printed material you must cope with. Business letters, monographs, report forms, memoranda, trade journals, perhaps textbooks, theses, all types of collateral reading for your business or school work; not to mention newspapers, advertisements, and all the novels, short stories, and magazines which you would *like* to read but never have the time for. The list could go on and on.

The fact is that our society has become increasingly dependent on the printed page as the basic medium for mass communication. There is more and more material in print every day, and more and more people, including you, have to read it. The flood of print threatens to drown us all, unless we can find the secret of faster, better reading.

The problem may at first glance appear insoluble; yet, it is not. Your reading need not be a burden; you simply must learn how to handle it.

Whenever the modern world has made new demands upon us, modern methods have been found to deal with them. This is just as true for reading. In only ten days you can learn the modern techniques for reading—in *half the time* with *more comprehension!* If you will spend just a few minutes a day for the next ten days with this book, you will master your reading load. You will improve your vocabulary. You will learn the modern techniques of phrase reading, space reading, indentation, skimming, columnar reading, pre-reading, critical reading, and many others. In fact, your reading will improve by 10 per cent or more on the *very first day!* All that is necessary on your part is the wish to improve and the determination to practice.

Now stop timing yourself.—STOP—How long did it take you? Probably at least a minute—which means you have a reading rate of less than 300 words per minute. (225-250 wpm is average for an intelligent American adult.) You can double this rate in the next ten days. You will learn to apply your faster, more effective reading rate to newspapers, textbooks and business materials. Your new rate will enable you to get swiftly to the core of the article or book you are reading, to evaluate the central idea, to recognize details as such, and to spot faulty and inconsistent reasoning processes. You will, in short, become a rapid and effective reader.

All it takes is practice. In the ten days you set for yourself you must practice the new techniques not only for the few minutes necessary to complete the exercises in this book, but with *everything that you read.* And on the very first day you will be able to *see* your reading load shrink.

PART ONE

Reading Techniques

Reading can be seen as a two-part process involving the relationship between the reader's eye and the printed page, and the connection between the reader's eye and his mind. The first can be seen as mechanical; the second is mental since it entails evaluation of the material.

Eye-Page Relationship

Phrase Reading

When your eyes move across a line, they do not travel in a single smooth sweep, but in a series of stops and starts called "eye fixations." The more eye fixations you make on a single line, the longer it takes you to read.

The first reading technique, "phrase reading," is designed to allow you to cut down on the number of eye fixations per line, to take in words in bigger "visual bites" or thought-units.

Sample:

Do	you	read	word	by	word
or	can you read		phrase by phrase		

Remember that individual words are rarely significant in themselves, but take on meaning only in context or in word-groups. Therefore, the reader who sees words in thought-units is already two steps ahead of the game; he reads faster because he has cut down on eye fixations, and he understands more easily because he is reading in terms of concepts and thoughts rather than by individual words.

Space Reading

The best way to train your eyes to read phrases is to practice "space reading." That is, rather than focusing your eyes directly on the print, *lift* them so they focus slightly above the line; allow your eyes to relax and "spread" your span of vision over several words, so that you are reading a whole phrase at a time, not a single word.

Bound into this book there is a special phrase card. Use it to check on your present eye movements. In the center of the card is a small circle. Cut this out to make a hole. Then have someone hold the card about fourteen inches from your eyes and look through the hole while you read one side of the card. He will be able to see the eye movements that you make as you read. Have him check for the number of eye movements that you make as you read the card. The upper left-hand portion of the card is to be cut out and used as a mask for phrase-reading practice. Below is a sample list of phrases.

once and for all
feel the need to
What time is it?
he had witnessed
being in fashion.
The sky is clear.
college   education
take   advantage   of
bigger   and   better
get   along   without
a   brighter   future
a   small   number   of
almost   as   much   as
from   bad   to   worse
be   that   as   it   may
standard   practice
the   importance   of

Use the special card to practice phrase reading on this list. After you have finished this exercise, have the other person check your eye movements again to see how much you have improved. Also, use the edge of the card as a pacing device. Draw it down the page at a faster pace than you normally read in order to establish a comfortable rhythm in your phrase reading.

Pacing

When your partner checked your eye movements, he may have caught you at another bad habit which slows down the great majority of readers—the habit of *needless regressions*. If you have not completely understood what you have read, it is, of course, necessary to go back and check the meaning. But too many readers have an almost unconscious habit of frequently regressing on a line even though they have thoroughly understood its meaning. The phrase reader must eliminate this habit by practicing smooth, rhythmic eye swings across the line. Constant practice with the special card as a pacing device will put an end to the time wasted by needless regressions.

Phrase Marking

By focusing above the line of print rather than directly on it, you have been able to take bigger "visual bites" from the page. This is the first step on the road to becoming an efficient phrase reader. Now, it is absolutely necessary that you read not only by word groups, but by *meaningful* word groups. Look for the units of thought. To increase your awareness of phrases, practice phrase marking. As you read the rest of this section of the book, analyze the print in terms of meaningful phrases or thought-units, and *box* each thought-unit with your pencil. With this simple technique you will quickly develop a clear awareness of logical phrase structure.

15

Example:

Phrase marking is / a useful technique

for increasing awareness / of phrase structure

that you should practice / for five minutes

a day / for the next / ten days

Indentation

The techniques of space reading and phrase marking have helped you become a faster reader, but you are probably still not making the most of your reading time. It's surprising, but true, that most people spend as much as 20 to 30 per cent of their time reading *margins*. When you begin to read a line of print, you will tend to make your first eye fixation on the first word of a line; when you finish the line, you will tend to stop on the last word. Since we have already ascertained that you have a definite span of vision, it follows that when you focus on the first word of a line, *half* of your vision span is in the margin, reading *blank space*. The same holds true at the end of a line.

In other words, you are in the position of the driver who wastes gas by racing his motor in neutral gear. It doesn't get him anywhere. To read efficiently, you must practice *indenting* on a line. Begin your eye fixations two or three words within the line of print—as much as your vision or span of recognition will permit. When you finish a line, make your last eye fixation two or three words from the end. Never skip words, but read *nothing but words*. It is often helpful to draw two light lines down each side of the page to act as guides for your initial and final eye fixations. Following is a sample page with guidelines already marked for you to use for practice.

WHEN THE PRESIDENT DECIDES *

In the mid-twentieth century the President of the United States is the acknowledged leader of the free world. His prestige derives not alone from that central role which America plays today in world affairs but also from the nature of the unique office of the Presidency, the traditions that have gathered about that office, and the way its occupants have wielded their powers. Despite its world significance the Presidency is in essence an American institution shaped by the forces of American history. Not inaccurately has the President been described as a kind of "one-man distillation of the American people." The office has constituted a great challenge to those who have won election to it. The Presidency has seemed to endow even average men with unexpected wisdom and strength, with a willingness to place country above narrow partisan considerations and to exercise effective powers in times of crisis. The Presidency is a standing refutation to those who have criticized democracy on the ground that it cannot decide promptly nor act with vigor. This book documents that refutation.

Indentation is an integral part of phrase reading. Practice indentation on everything that you read.

Columnar Reading

When you have become fairly proficient at indentation, you will be able to try columnar reading. Take a column of a newspaper or magazine, draw a light line down the center of it and practice moving your eyes down the guideline, *reading each line with a single eye fixation.* Below is a sample column already marked for your practice. Practice this technique as much as possible—always

*Richard B. Morris, *Great Presidential Decisions* (Greenwich, Conn.: Fawcett Publications, Inc., Premier Book M131, 1961), p. 9.

trying to increase your visual span by choosing wider and wider columns.

> My paramount object in this struggle is to save the Union, and is not either to save or destroy slavery. If I could save the Union without freeing any slaves, I would do it; and if I could save it by freeing all the slaves, I would do it; and if I could save it by freeing some and leaving others alone, I would also do that. What I do about slavery and the colored race, I do because I believe it helps to save the Union; and what I forbear, I forbear because I do not believe it would help to save the Union. . . .
> I have here stated my purpose according to my view of official duty; and I intend no modification of my oft-expressed personal wish that all men everywhere could be free.*

Key-Word Reading

Once you are an accomplished phrase reader, and, on a particular article, desire a more thorough comprehension than pre-reading will provide, yet do not want to read the article thoroughly, you will find a technique called *key-word reading* perfectly adapted to your needs. Run your eyes over the page in a rhythmic zigzag motion. Your awareness of phrases will allow you to stop at the key phrases that contain the pith of the article. The following samples are key-word and eye-swing exercises for your practice. Eye-swing exercises will help you develop a smooth phrase-reading rhythm.

*A letter from Abraham Lincoln to Horace Greeley, Richard B. Morris, *op. cit.*, p. 252

By the President of the United States
A PROCLAMATION*

Whereas existing exigencies demand immediate and adequate measures for the protection of the National Constitution and the preservation of the National Union by the suppression of the insurrectionary combinations now existing in several States for opposing the laws of the Union and obstructing the execution thereof, to which end a military force in addition to that called forth by my proclamation of the 15th day of April in the present year appears to be indispensably necessary:

Now, therefore, I, Abraham Lincoln, President of the United States and Commander in Chief of the Army and Navy thereof and of the militia of the several States when called into actual service, do hereby call into the service of the United States 42,034 volunteers to serve for the period of three years, unless sooner discharged, and to be mustered into service as infantry and cavalry. The proportions of each arm and the details of enrollment and organization will be made known through the Department of War.

Reading these paragraphs according to the key words, you would see:

                    exigencies demand
    measures   protection   Con-
stitution   preservation   Union
    suppression of the insurrectionary combinations
        in   States   opposing
Union

              I, Abraham Lincoln,

                                    call into the service
            42,034 volunteers

*Richard B. Morris, *op. cit.*, p. 248

Eye-Swing

This exercise will help you to develop a smooth reading rhythm and to reduce the number of stops your eyes make on each line of print. "Read" the exercise by glancing briefly at each solid bar. Keep on "reading" rapidly or you may find yourself making more than two fixations on each line. Be sure to make fast, even swings from the end of one line to the beginning of the next. One "reading" at a time is enough—but keep practicing every day.

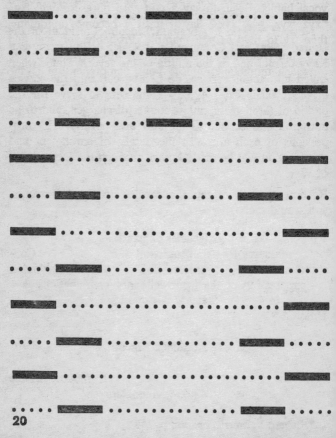

Mumbling

There is yet another way to make phrase reading serve you better. Even though you may be able to *see* meaningful word groups with a single eye fixation, you may tend to *say each word* to yourself or *hear* each individual word as you read. Obviously, if you persist in your vocal or auditory habits, you will be greatly reducing the benefits that can be derived from phrase reading.

The technique of *mumbling* will eradicate auditory and vocal habits. Begin to say a nonsense phrase *aloud,* e.g., "xyz, xyz, xyz, xyz." Say it until it becomes automatic, then try to read as you mumble. Probably you will find that your comprehension is seriously affected. The degree to which mumbling reduces your comprehension is the degree to which you depend on your auditory or vocal organs to read. The good reader reads almost entirely by sight. He does not have to translate the print into sounds in order to understand it. Mumbling would not affect his comprehension, since, for him, reading is a visual operation. If you practice the mumbling technique for at least ten minutes a day for the next ten days, you will have taken a big step toward becoming a sight reader, rather than one who "talks" his way through print.

Here, then, are some ... that will...
... two or three ...
... you... that you are... there...

Eye-Mind Relationship

Pre-Reading

Phrase reading has enabled you to read according to the logical structure of language. You have been reading according to the meaning of the language, that is, reading in thought-units. The modern reader, however, must also be able to read according to the *logical structure of the book or article* he is reading. The modern reader *pre-reads* every piece of factual prose before he actually reads it.

Pre-reading is a technique that will help you to grasp the "bony structure" of an article or book—to get a rapid overview of its contents in terms of main idea, author's thesis, style, and approach. By spotting the author's conclusions and reasoning processes beforehand, you can direct your reading and know just what to look for in order to get the best comprehension most rapidly. Another advantage of pre-reading is that it will often allow you to discard useless material without wasting your time in a thorough reading.

Articles

Pre-read magazine articles, newspaper editorials, and news commentaries by quickly looking at the title and the author of the piece, then reading the first two or three paragraphs to get an introduction to the topic under discussion. Read the first sentence of each subsequent paragraph to perceive the development of the author's thesis, then read the final paragraph or two for his conclusions. With practice you should be able to pre-read a full-length magazine article in less than two minutes. When you decide to go ahead and read the article thoroughly after pre-reading, you will find that your total reading time will be much less than if you had tried to read the article thoroughly from a cold start.

Texts

Pre-read business reports and textbooks by reading bold print, maps, graphs, and summary statements that are furnished for you. Your pre-reading approach will, of course, vary according to the typography of the particular textbook or business report you are reading, but remember that this type of material is *written to be pre-read*. That is why the bold print and other visual aids are there, so make use of them for your overview.

Books

Pre-read entire books by reading the foreword, introduction, preface, any introductory or concluding chapters, table of contents and index.

News Stories

Pre-read news stories by reading the headlines and the first two or three paragraphs only. A critic's opinion in a book or drama review is almost always contained in the last two paragraphs.

Of course, you should never pre-read fiction, but you must form the habit of pre-reading *every* piece of factual material you encounter. Only through constant practice can pre-reading become the habit it should be—a quick, automatic once-over that provides a big boost to your reading efficiency. Following is a demonstration of how easily an article can be pre-read. Note the italics.

Sample Pre-Reading Exercise

By the middle of the nineteenth century the march of Manifest Destiny was converting America into a Pacific power. President Fillmore had shown admirable restraint in refusing to be a party to a rather shady proposal to annex Hawaii; yet he recognized the importance to Americans of this mid-Pacific island chain and was determined that it should not come under the control of any other great power. To Congress he predicted that "at no distant day" a "great trade" would be carried on between the American West Coast and eastern Asia.

Trade with China was already burgeoning. Japan, which exercised a marvelous fascination for Americans, lay athwart the direct route between San Francisco and Shanghai. Not only was the United States interested in protecting shipwrecked whalers who found the Japanese coast hitherto inhospitable, but it was considered imperative that the Navy and Merchant Marine have coaling stations along the Japanese archipelago, as ships were shifting from sail to steam. But Japan remained sealed off to the western world save for special concessions which the Dutch enjoyed under humiliating conditions.

From time to time enterprising Yankee sea captains had defied the boycott of the hated foreigners, but nevertheless found it impossible to raise the bamboo curtain which cut the native Japanese off from contact with the West. George Cleveland, who actually landed goods in Japan as early as 1801, reported: "No person in this country (who has not traded with people who have so little intercourse with the world) can have an idea of the trouble we had in delivering the little Invoice." Other contacts were casual. As late as 1846 an American expedition under Commodore Biddle visited Yedo, only to find the port closed. President Fillmore was determined to keep trade routes open to the Far East and to expand trans-Pacific commerce and communications. Late in 1850 he transferred Commodore Aulick from the South Atlantic command to the East India squadron, and, in the words of Secretary of State Daniel Webster's instructions, it was stated as "the President's opinion, that steps should be taken at once to enable our enterprising merchants to supply the last link in that great chain which unites all nations of the world by the establishment of a line of steamers from California to China." Webster pointed out the desirability of obtaining supplies of coal from the subjects of the Emperor of Japan, a matter which continued to be on Fillmore's mind. The Aulick mission never got under way because the Commodore was involved in an incident which made him unacceptable for diplomatic duty.

Fillmore and Webster now decided to give the mission a more imposing aspect by sending out an independent fleet under the command of Matthew Calbraith Perry, selected to undertake the most important diplomatic mission ever entrusted to an American naval officer—the negotiation of a treaty with Japan. In preparing a message to the Emperor Fillmore was puzzled about the correct protocol to be employed. He had the American minister to the Netherlands secure from the Dutch foreign office the reply of the shogun in 1844 to an address by William II asking that ports be opened to foreign trade. Fillmore discarded the first draft, and on Webster's death his successor, Edward Everett, prepared a second one, which seems to have been the basis for Fillmore's final letter. A Dutch physician named von Siebold, "the self-constituted court chamberlain of Japan," criticized President Fillmore for being "wanting in the courtly proprieties of diplomatic etiquette," but these are minor flaws in a state paper simply but artfully conceived, whose far-reaching impact may still be felt.

The letter was presented in a ceremony on July 14, 1853, on shore at the village of Kurihama. Commodore Perry was preceded by two boys, dressed for the ceremony, bearing in an envelope of scarlet cloth the boxes which contained his credentials and the President's letter, both written on vellum and bound in blue silk velvet. The documents were delivered to the princes Idzu and Iwami, representatives of the Emperor, in an interview which lasted no more than half an hour. *His Imperial Highness,* correct protocol or not, got the point of Fillmore's letter, responded through his commissioners in a friendly manner, and *on March 31, 1854, made a treaty with the United States granting trade rights at the two ports of Hakodate and Shinoda. The bamboo curtain had at long last been lifted.**

From pre-reading, you should have a mental picture of the "bony structure" of the article:

I. Desires of Americans to make further contacts with Far East

II. Unsuccessful overtures to Japan by Yankee traders

III. Fillmore sends fleet under Perry

IV. Emperor agrees to a U.S.-Japanese treaty

*Richard B. Morris, *op. cit.*, p. 192-194

Skimming

Many people spend a great deal of their reading time trying to find a *specific bit of information*. Rather than wading through page after page of material until you find what you are looking for, you can save a tremendous amount of time by utilizing the technique of *skimming*. If you know exactly what you are looking for, run your eyes down the center of the page *without reading*. The particular fact you want, if it is on the page at all, will seem to jump right out at you. Some skilled readers prefer to skim by running their eyes diagonally over the page, first from the upper left-hand corner to the lower right-hand corner, then from the upper right-hand corner to the lower left-hand corner.

Concentration

External Conditions

In order to apply the techniques discussed so far with any degree of efficiency, it is absolutely necessary to *concentrate* as you read. You must first be sure that you are reading under the proper *external conditions* for maximum concentration. Avoid fatigue. Never read for several hours without a break. Read in a good light—at least a 100-watt bulb with one other light in the room to avoid glare. Hold the book about fourteen inches from your eyes and in a position where the print at the bottom of the page will be the same distance from your eyes as the print at the top of the page. Have your eyes checked regularly. Never read in a sprawled position in a too-soft chair. A hard chair with a desk to support the book is best. A slight, regular background noise is better than absolute silence, for it raises your whole level of concentration. And finally, it is useless to read when you are bothered by pressing emotional or business problems: your mind must be free of extraneous worry before you can start any serious reading project.

Question and Anticipate

Get yourself in the right *mental* state to concentrate. Most concentration difficulties stem from the fact that the mind is not occupied by the reading at hand, and is easily distracted. *Question* and *anticipate* to become an *active* reader, to keep your mind busy. Before you even start to pre-read, begin to organize your past experience around the article. What do you know about the topic? How do you think the author will approach the subject? What do you know about the author himself? As you pre-read be constantly on the alert to perceive the author's thesis, and distinguish it from his reasoning processes. Who? What? Where? When? Why? and How? are your "faithful serving men," and you should be constantly trying to provide them with answers. As you read thoroughly, it is useful to turn the topic sentence of each paragraph into a question and try to answer it from the rest of the paragraph. An example is given below.

Sample Question Exercise

Some of these decisions had immediate impact. Washington's proclamation against the Whisky Insurrection, for example, was followed by a swift show of force against the rebels; Truman's announcement that the United States would come to the aid of the Korean Republic signaled the start of a "police action" which involved the lives of countless soldiers and threatened the entire world with the spectre of World War III.*

If you turn the topic sentence into a question, it reads: "Which of these decisions had immediate impact?" By reading the rest of the paragraph, you find the answers to your question. Reading should be done in short spurts of high-geared mental activity. If you don't give your mind a chance to be distracted, you will never have any concentration difficulties.

*Richard B. Morris, *op. cit.*, p. 1

Cue Words

The more alert you are to *cue words,* the better equipped you will be to anticipate and question. Cue words like IN ADDITION TO, THEREFORE, FOR THIS REASON, IN BRIEF, IN CONCLUSION, TO SUM UP, ALTHOUGH, BUT, NEVERTHELESS, ON THE CONTRARY, IN PARTICULAR, SPECIFICALLY, etc., indicate important thoughts to come, or major shifts in the author's development of his thesis. For the next ten days, be very conscious of cue words and try to spot them in everything that you read. After ten days of this kind of practice, you will read for cue words automatically.

Summarizing

Summarizing not only helps concentration, but is also a valuable comprehension device. As you finish each major section of a particular reading, jot down very briefly its main idea, and list in outline form any major and necessary details. A few minutes spent summarizing can save you hours of restudying and rereading. Save and file summaries of all the important reading you do—that way you can never forget what you have read.

Critical Reading

Everything we have discussed so far is useless unless you are also a *critical reader.* You must do more than merely comprehend what you read; you must be able to *test* it as well. Approach everything with a healthy skepticism; accept nothing as truth merely because it is printed. Never confuse fact with opinion. A fact is usually a scientifically observable phenomenon; an opinion is what the author *thinks* is true but cannot necessarily prove. Jot down the author's reasoning process in outline form, so that any flaws in his logical chain will stand out in bas-relief. Beware of emotional or evocative language. Never allow an author's feelings to run away with *your* good sense.

Note-Taking

Becoming a better reader will make you a better and more alert *listener* and *note-taker* as well. In the lecture hall or the conference room it is essential that you listen and take notes on *main ideas* rather than try to copy down everything that is said, that you summarize mentally as you listen, that you question and anticipate, and that you be just as critical as you are when you read. Don't forget that it is much easier for a forceful person to influence you by speaking to you than by writing to you—so, more than ever, be on your guard against fallacious or misleading arguments.

Supplementary Exercises

For the next ten days, in order to sharpen yourself, you will also be working on vocabulary exercises, paragraph development, sentence correction and completion, and visualizing and direction-following.

Vocabulary

These exercises stress recognition of basic word roots, derivation of meaning from prefixes and suffixes, and use of words in context. The roots chosen are fundamental to a strong vocabulary and will also provide a basis for learning thousands of new words in addition to those included in the exercises. A sample exercise is given below.

Sample Vocabulary Exercise

For instance, nothing can be more incredible than the mercenary conduct of Corvino, in delivering up his wife to the palsied embraces of Volpone; and yet the poet does not seem in the least to boggle at the incongruity of it . . .*

incredible—unbelievable.
     From Latin *in* (not) + *credibilis* (believable).

What are the definitions of the following words? Be sure to check them in your dictionary.
     credence
     creed
     credible
     credulity
     credulous
     incredulity
     incredulous

*Herschel M. Sikes, ed., *The Hazlitt Sampler* (Greenwich, Conn.: Fawcett Publications, Inc., Premier Book t132, 1961), p. 21.

mercenary—motivated by desire for money or gain.

From Latin *merces* (pay, wages, reward).

What are the definitions of the following words? Be sure to check them in your dictionary.

mercantile
mercantilism
mercenarily
mercenariness
merchandise
merchant

incongruity—state of not corresponding, not being in agreement.

From Latin *in* (not) + *con* (with) + *gruens* (agreeing).

What are the definitions and *roots* of the following words? Be sure and check them in your dictionary.

conflict
conform
confrere
confront
congenial
congregate
congruence
congruent
congruity
congruous
incongruence
incongruent
incongruous
conjugate
connubial
consequent

Practice on these exercises will definitely help you along the road to rapid and efficient phrase reading. They emphasize *accuracy* of word perception and an understanding of the relationship of individual words to over-all meaning. An awareness of the structure and logic of language is a prerequisite for the phrase reader. Samples of each are given below.

Sample Sentence Completion and Correction Exercises

Fill in the following blanks:

Nearly 12,500,000 people in the United States today own common stock. This fact, so briefly stated, is of first-rank _____. For it _____ one of the profound and far-reaching shifts in American social and economic life in the twentieth century. _____ before in our history have so _____ of us owned so _____ of the nation's industrial wealth. . . .*
(*Answers on p. 170*)

Find the illogical word:

When we turn . . . to the cities, the uniformity is even more remarkable. With five or six exceptions, . . . American cities are alike only herein, that some are built more with brick than with wood, and others more with wood than with brick.†

*Adolph Suehsdorf, *How To Invest Safely and For Profit* (Greenwich, Conn.: Fawcett Publications, Inc., Crest Book d376, 1960), p. 9.

†James Bryce, *Reflections on American Institutions* (Greenwich, Conn.: Fawcett Publications, Inc., Premier Book t140, 1961), p. 217.

Paragraph Development

Good pre-reading is based on rapid perception of paragraph structure and meaning. These exercises will be an invaluable aid in the development of that skill. A sample is given below.

Sample Paragraph Development Exercise

Arrange the following sentences* in their proper order. What is the topic sentence of the paragraph?

1) The swindlers, operating illegally, or, at best, at the barest edge of legality, are not inclined to report their profits.
2) But one classic swindle, alone, engineered in the past year or so, mulcted the suckers for $16 million, and its promoter was by no means the only operator in the field.
3) Exactly how many millions is not known.
4) Stock swindlers fleece investors out of millions of dollars every year.
5) The victims, beating their foreheads in humiliation, are hesitant to confess their stupidity.

(*Answers on p. 170*)

Visual Aids and Direction-Following

The accomplished reader must be able to mentally transpose printed material into clear and meaningful patterns. These exercises are designed to develop this skill. See the sample below.

Sample Visualizing and Direction-Following Exercise

Read next paragraph on the following page and then draw the experiment:

*Adolph Suehsdorf, *op. cit.*, p. 195

Place an iron shot of three or four inches diameter on the mouth of a clean, dry glass bottle. By a fine silken thread from the ceiling, right over the mouth of the bottle, suspend a small cork ball, about the bigness of a marble; the thread of such a length, as that the cork ball may rest against the side of the shot. Electrify the shot, and the ball will be repelled to the distance of four or five inches, more or less, according to the quantity of electricity. When in this state, if you present to the shot the point of a long slender sharp bodkin [metal needle], at six or eight inches distance, the repellency is instantly destroyed and the cork flies to the shot.*

Draw the experiment:

*Nathan G. Goodman, ed., *The Benjamin Franklin Sampler* (Greenwich, Conn.: Fawcett Publications, Inc., Premier Book s31, 1956), p. 132.

PART TWO

Now that you have read and understood
this much, you can start your TEN DAYS to
swifter, more accurate reading.

Day I

Phrase Reading

Following is the first *phrase reading* exercise. The selection below is broken into logical phrase groups. Read the selection *at least three times,* making a *single eye stop* on each phrase group. Remember to keep your eyes relaxed. If you strain to widen your effective vision span, more often than not you will only succeed in narrowing it. Focus your eyes slightly above the line of print rather than directly on it. Take your time the first time through the selection, and increase your speed the second and third time.

Phrase Reading Exercise #1

She was awakened   by a shock   so sudden   and severe   that if Dorothy   had not been lying   on the soft bed   she might have   been hurt.   As it was,   the jar   made her catch   her breath and wonder   what had happened;   and Toto put his cold little nose   into her face   and whined dismally.   Dorothy sat up   and noticed   that the house   was not moving;   nor was it dark,   for the bright sunshine   came in   at the window, flooding   the little room.   She sprang   from her bed   and with Toto   at her heels   ran and opened the door.

The little girl   gave a cry   of amazement and looked   about her,   her eyes   growing bigger   and bigger   at the wonderful sights   she saw.   The cyclone   had set   the house down very gently—   for a cyclone—   in the midst of a country   of marvelous beauty.*

*L. Frank Baum, *The Wizard of Oz* (Greenwich, Conn.: Fawcett Publications, Inc., Crest Book K674, 1960), pp. 19-20.

Indenting

Indenting is a time-saving skill that follows logically from *phrase reading*. Since the average reader has the habit of making the initial and final eye fixations on the first and last word of a line, he wastes a great deal of his eye span in the margins. The following selection has guidelines drawn for your first and last eye stops. Follow the guidelines to improve your skill in *indenting*. Do the exercise at least three times, or until *indenting* seems natural.

Indenting Exercise #1

On the Gulf side of these islands you may observe that the trees—when there are any trees—all bend away from the sea; and, even of bright, hot days when the wind sleeps, there is something grotesquely pathetic in their look of agonized terror. A group of oaks at Grande Isle I remember as especially suggestive: five stooping silhouettes in line against the horizon, like fleeing women with streaming garments and wind-blown hair,—bowing grievously and thrusting out arms desperately northward as to save themselves from falling. And they are being pursued indeed;—for the sea is devouring the land. Many and many a mile of ground has yielded to the tireless charging of Ocean's cavalry: far out you can see, through a good glass, the porpoises at play where of old the sugar-cane shook out its million bannerets; and shark-fins now seam deep water above a site where pigeons used to coo. Men build dikes; but the besieging tides bring up their battering-rams—whole forests of drift —huge trunks of water-oak and weighty cypress. Forever the yellow Mississippi strives to build; forever the sea struggles to destroy. . . . *

---

*Lafcadio Hearn, *Chita* (Greenwich, Conn.: Fawcett Publications, Inc., Premier Book D135, 1961), p. 25.

Eye Swing

The ophthalmograph (an electronic device for recording eye movements) shows that the average reader uses extremely *inefficient, ragged* eye movements across a line of print. The skilled reader, on the other hand, has a smooth, rhythmic *eye swing*. Use the following exercise to develop the pattern of your eye movements. Make one eye-stop on each heavy black mark. Move your eyes as rapidly as possible. Do the exercise for no more than three minutes.

Eye-Swing Exercise #1

Key-Word Reading

This is your first *key-word reading* exercise. Key-word reading is the ability to spot the important words in a selection, those relatively few words that carry most of the meaning. In the selection below, circle the key words as you read. Don't spend time mulling over your choices, however; do the exercise as rapidly as possible. Key-word reading is essentially a speed skill.

"WILLIAM RANDOLPH, gentleman, of Turkey Island," born in 1650, was a native of Warwickshire in England, as his tombstone declares. Of his ancestry nothing is certainly known. The cause and the time of his coming to Virginia have been forgotten. The Henrico records show that in 1678 he was clerk of Henrico County, a man of substance, and married already to Mary Isham; that in 1685 he was "Captain William Randolph" and Justice of the Peace; that in 1706 he conveyed to son Henry "land called by the name of Curles, with Longfield," being all that land at "Curles" lately belonging to Nathaniel Bacon, Jr.; that in 1709 "Col. William Randolph of Turkey Island" made his will, which mentioned seven sons and two daughters; and finally that in 1711 he died.*

Here is what you should have:

"WILLIAM RANDOLPH,   Turkey Island,"
born   1650,   native   Warwickshire   England,
                                        ancestry nothing
        known.   cause   time   coming
   Virginia   forgotten.
            1678   clerk   Henrico County,
man   substance,   married   Mary Isham;
       1685   "Captain
Justice   Peace;   1706   to son
       "land   name   Curles,
                                     lately belonging

Nathaniel Bacon, Jr.;   1709 "Col.

seven sons   two daughters;   1711
died.

*Henry Adams, *John Randolph* (Greenwich, Conn.: Fawcett Publications, Inc., Premier Book d139, 1961), p. 19.

Sentence Completion and Inference

Another exercise to increase your skill with words and to develop your ability to discern thought patterns as you read is the *sentence completion and inference* exercise. From the information given in the following selections, you are to infer what words should appear in the blanks, and complete the selections.

Sentence Completion Exercise #1

A—America has always been a land of _____. Whatever the course of our economy in the years immediately _____, it is likely that _____ for investment will be both numerous and attractive. Energetic _____ companies will emerge, looking for _____ capital. Solid _____ companies will come forth with exciting new products. One industry or another will enjoy a boom period relative to the rest. And, of course, there will be _____, too. There inevitably are.*

(*Answers on p. 170*)

B—For the _____ investor, this activity, properly evaluated and properly timed, will bring _____. There will be chances to buy stocks before they have called attention to themselves and begun to _____, or to buy a blue chip, temporarily out of _____ at a _____ price. There will be stock splits, dividend increases, new issues, mergers, spin-offs, as well as the tidal _____ and _____ of stock prices—all of this _____ of the restless life of market as a _____ of American business.*

(*Answers on p. 170*)

*Adolph Suehsdorf, *op. cit.*, p. 19

How to Read Your Newspaper

"Nothing is staler than yesterday's news" is an old and trite saying, perhaps, but one that contains a great deal of truth. Even a newspaperman will usually admit that his writing is essentially transitory. Except for an occasional Pulitzer Prize-winning story, a news story is read for the facts it contains on a certain day. By the next day the facts have changed, and the original story has lost its relevancy. So a reporter's or an editor's prime concern is to present facts in the most clear, concise, and readable fashion possible without much of an eye to literary merit. The AP, for instance, at one time had a standing rule that no story could contain more than an average nineteen words per sentence; that no paragraph could contain more than three sentences; that, in general, all polysyllabic words were to be avoided when a monosyllable would express the sense as well. As a matter of fact, almost all newspapers, with one or two notable exceptions, are written with a sixth-grade readership level in mind. All of this is not calculated as an affront to the intelligence of the reader, but simply as the newspapers' way of meeting an existing demand; since a newspaper, by its very nature, is doomed to be read in a scanning, perfunctory way, it is written to accommodate such a reading.

Since the newspapers are trying to accommodate *you*, take advantage of the journalistic style to the hilt. Scan the headlines to pick out the articles that interest you most. Then, when you read the articles themselves, keep the inverted-pyramid style of presentation in mind, and adjust

43

your reading rate accordingly. Inverted-pyramid style simply means that all the important facts will be presented in the first paragraph or two, and that each succeeding paragraph will be of progressively less importance. The inverted-pyramid is a style peculiar to newspapers and stems from the fact that a reporter writing for a wire service has no idea where the various editors will cut his story to fit their papers. Thus, he writes his stories so that no matter how much is cut off the bottom of the column, the facts will still be there and will still make sense. Except for the one or two major stories of the day (usually on the right-hand side of the front page), you will usually find that a glance at the headline and the first two paragraphs of each article will suffice to keep you up on the news.

After reading the news stories on the first two or three pages, turn to the editorial pages. This section will present quite a different reading situation. First of all, since less than twenty per cent of the readers even bother to read the editorials, they are usually aimed at the most thoughtful, perceptive, and intelligent segment of the public and, although clarity is still at a premium, they are apt to be more difficult and elevated in content, language, and style than the rest of the paper. Secondly, while news stories are essentially expository in nature, that is, concerned with presenting facts and facts alone, editorials are essentially *persuasive*. They are trying to sell something—either a point of view or a mode of action. The same holds true for the columnists and analysts whose comments on world or local affairs will appear in the editorial section. They have a point of view; they are trying to convince you of something. Don't be too skeptical, however; editorials and analytic columns are written by intelligent men whose business it is to understand and try to help others to understand the events that are shaping the world. In this sense perhaps more than in any other, the newspapers perform a valuable service. The editorials and columns deserve a thorough, thoughtful reading. Pre-read them first. Compare their analysis of the events of the last few days (their comments will usually be on yesterday's

44

news) with your own. But don't make the mistake of accepting their word as gospel. When you read them thoroughly, read them critically as well. When there is a political issue under discussion, for instance, it is the publisher of the paper who will dictate the party line to be followed, and the editorials will follow that line. As a thoughtful reader, it is up to you to discern the stand the paper is taking. Read the editorials every day, compare each day's comments to the previous day's, discover the trend of a particular paper's thinking. Is it conservative or liberal in domestic politics? What about international affairs —isolationist or cosmopolitan? Business or labor? Does it adhere to strictly partisan lines, or will it take an independent position and switch from side to side according to the merit of the particular issues in question? Whom do you expect it to endorse in the next local or national elections? Why?

In any large city, you will usually be able to find two newspapers which take consistently opposite stands on most issues. Subscribe to them both to get a complete picture of events. But always remember—draw your own conclusions.

The news section and the editorial pages are the heart of any paper. After them, there is little else except sports, the entertainment section, comics, and advertisements. Read the latter at your leisure—any way you prefer or have the time for, but remember, those five or six pages —the news and the editorials—are the real reason for the newspaper's existence. Make time for them.

On the following page is a sample news article that demonstrates the "inverted-pyramid" style of construction.

Kennedy Picks Wirtz to Head Labor Dept.

Goldberg Appointed To High Court as Frankfurter Retires

By ROBERT ROTH

Bulletin Washington Bureau

Washington, Aug. 30—President Kennedy today named W. Willard Wirtz as secretary of labor to succeed Arthur J. Goldberg, who was nominated yesterday as an associate justice of the Supreme Court.

The cabinet post became vacant when the President nominated Goldberg to succeed Justice Felix Frankfurter, who is retiring because of ill health.

Mr. Kennedy announced his selection of Wirtz after a brief White House conference this morning with AFL-CIO president George Meany. Wirtz, 50, has been serving as under secretary of labor.

FORMER STEVENSON PARTNER

The appointment came as no surprise. Wirtz, formerly a law partner of United Nations Ambassador Adlai Stevenson, was known to rank high in the esteem of both the President and Goldberg and his name led all others in advance speculation as to a possible successor for Goldberg.

In negotiations over labor disputes affecting the national interest, Wirtz several times drew the commendation of both labor and management spokesmen.

Wirtz got word of his appointment in Chicago, where he is acting as mediator in a railroad strike. Goldberg was in Chicago yesterday on the same mission when he received a message telling him he had become a Supreme Court justice.

Mr. Kennedy called newsmen to a special conference to announce the Wirtz selection.*

Notice how in the above article all the important information—whom Kennedy appointed, to what, and whom the man is succeeding—is contained in the first paragraph. The second paragraph is slightly less important and the rest, except, perhaps, for the background of Wirtz, is almost nonessential.

*From *The Evening Bulletin*, Philadelphia, Aug. 30, 1962.

Day II

Phrase Reading Exercise #2

After a time, the strained and wary courtesy of their manners wore away. It became evident to Bleeker that his importance slightly dazzled the young man. He grew warmer. Obviously, the youth was one whose powers of perception were developed. Directly, then, he launched forth into a tale of bygone days when the world was better. He had known all the great men of that age. He reproduced his conversations with them. There were traces of pride and of mournfulness in his voice. He rejoiced at the glory of the world of dead spirits. He grieved at the youth and flippancy of the present one. He lived with his head in the clouds of the past, and he seemed obliged to talk of what he saw there.*

Skipping and Skimming

No matter how fast a busy man can read, he still cannot afford to read thoroughly everything that he sees. Indeed, he would waste valuable time to do so. He must develop the skill of *skipping and skimming*. In the following exercises, a question appears before a sample reading selection. *Skim* to find the answer. Strive to complete each exercise in ten seconds or less.

*Stephen Crane, *Maggie: A Girl of the Streets* (Greenwich, Conn.: Fawcett Publications, Inc., Premier Book d103, 1960), p. 103.

Skipping and Skimming Exercise #1

Question: How does the following proposal take into consideration revenue losses from a tax cut?

Senator John Doe proposed yesterday that a bill providing for a five-billion-dollar tax cut benefiting both individuals and corporations be called to a vote immediately.

In an hour-long speech, the senator charged that the "timidity" of those opposing the bill could block the legislation indefinitely and hasten the oncome of "the worst recession in recent years."

The senator claimed the bill has already received "more than adequate study." He said that revenue losses to the government could be partially compensated for by closing the many loopholes existing under present tax laws.

Indenting Exercise #2

Thirty years ago, Last Island lay steeped in the enormous light of even such magical days. July was dying;—for weeks no fleck of cloud had broken the heaven's blue dream of eternity; winds held their breath; slow wavelets caressed the bland brown beach with a sound as of kisses and whispers. To one who found himself alone, beyond the limits of the village, and beyond the hearing of its voices,—the vast silence, the vast light, seemed full of weirdness. And these hushes, these transparencies, do not always inspire a causeless apprehension: they are omens sometimes—omens of coming tempest. Nature,—incomprehensible Sphinx!—before her mightiest bursts of rage, ever puts forth her divinest witchery, makes more manifest her awful beauty. . . .*

*Lafcadio Hearn, *op. cit.,* p. 34

Paragraph Development

A good reader is always a *thinking* reader. You must be constantly aware of the linguistic logic or the structure of what you read. In the following exercises, you are to rearrange the sentences, so that they make a logical paragraph. As you develop your skill in these paragraph development exercises, you will find an immediate improvement in your ability to discern the main idea and structure of paragraphs.

Paragraph Development Exercise #1

Rearrange the sentences* in the proper order. What is the topic sentence of each group?

A—

1. She could not see at the time that her victory had been too sweeping.
2. In their campaigns they had gained self-reliance at the same time that they had lost some of their respect for the fighting qualities of the British regular.
3. Great Britain emerged from the Seven Years War with her empire strong as ever before.
4. Her American colonists had played their own part in defeating the French.
5. Moreover, they no longer had the enemy at their back door to drive to the mother country for support.
6. She was mistress of the seas, of North America, of India.

(*Answers on p. 170*)

*Paul M. Angle, *A New Continent and a New Nation, Volume One—Selected from The American Reader* (Greenwich, Conn.: Fawcett Publications, Inc., Premier Book d92, 1960), p. 131.

B—

1. Pontiac's conspiracy had shown that even in North America colonial boundaries would have to be protected.
2. So the British ministers reasoned.
3. But when the Stamp Act was passed early in 1765, grumbling changed to forcible resistance.
4. From this expenditure the colonies would benefit, as they had benefited from the war just ended.
5. The cost of the war had been heavy, and the cost of defending the Empire would continue.
6. The Americans, used to trading as they pleased, regardless of laws to the contrary, were annoyed, but limited themselves to grumbling.
7. What could be fairer than that they should bear a share of the burden.
8. To that end, the enforcement of the various acts—the Navigation Act, the Sugar Act—was tightened.

(*Answers on p. 170*)

How to Read Your Magazine

The first point to consider in reading a magazine is how to choose your magazine. Make your choice of reading matter according to your purpose in reading—are you reading for entertainment or for information? One thing is fairly certain: you will get little of either entertainment or information from the "pulps." These magazines are named for the poor quality of paper that they use. Their non-fiction, if any, is usually cheaply sensational, while their fiction is rarely above the juvenile level. Pulp fiction writers are often paid by the word and make their living by grinding out great quantities of material without paying much attention to its quality. Most pulps are worth neither your time nor your money.

The so-called slicks and semi-slicks are next in order—again named for the type of paper that they use. *Redbook, Cosmopolitan,* and many others like them fall into this category. In times past, the emphasis in the slicks and semi-slicks was on entertaining though not particularly serious fiction and perhaps one or two topical essays. In recent years, however, there have been signs that this pattern is being exactly reversed, with the non-fiction—often of excellent quality—occupying the paramount position. Writers of non-fiction in the slicks and semi-slicks are competent professionals, usually with newspaper experience. Their prose is smooth and easy to read. Since their emphasis is always on clarity, you will find that pre-reading will very often tell you everything you need to know about slick non-fiction articles. In general, pre-read all the non-fiction articles and then select the one or two that seem to contain exceptional insight, and read those with care. These should be approached in much the same way that you approach newspaper editorials. Never forget that you are being sold on something; keep all of your critical faculties alert. Magazines, just as newspapers, will tend to form along partisan lines on certain national or international issues, and the articles that they print will conform to that line.

Slick fiction, on the other hand, can be taken much more lightly. The writers are competent and entertaining, but they usually have little to say of any lasting interest. Read slick fiction if you are interested in diversion, in taking your mind off the grimmer aspects of the day; but don't look for great literature.

Lastly, there are the "quality" magazines. Publications such as *Harper's* and the *Atlantic Monthly* consistently offer thought-provoking and penetrating fiction and non-fiction written by outstanding men and women in their fields. There are also many smaller publications, much more modestly endowed financially, such as the *Saturday Review, The Reporter, The Nation, The New Republic*, and the *National Review*, which, even though they are far less appealing to the eye than the slicks, offer extremely sophisticated and intelligent, although sometimes fiercely partisan, analyses of current events, the arts, literature, education, and so forth.

While it is unlikely that you will have the time to read *all* of the quality periodicals, at least one or two deserve your attention. Since the low-budget publications are written for a relatively small and well-defined audience, they are apt to take sides more readily and state their opinions more candidly (and more violently) than the newspapers. It is always interesting to compare the opinions of consistently liberal magazines such as *The New Republic* or *The Reporter* with the extremely conservative the *National Review*, for instance. Almost everything in the quality magazines should be pre-read and read thoughtfully and critically. As a matter of fact, you may wish to keep some of these magazines for future reference.

No list of magazines would be complete without the

How-To publications. You can be sure, if you look hard enough, that you will be able to find directions for almost any project from fixing an electric frying pan to building a yacht. Some of the publications will presume a certain amount of technical experience on your part, so your selections will depend largely on your needs and your background.

The following is from a magazine article* that appeared in a national publication during the Civil War centennial. Pre-read it and read it. Keep track of your reading time, and then answer the questions that follow it.

Who Fired the First Shot?

> *Ask any two Civil War historians "Who started the war?" and a controversy will almost inevitably result. Getting down to particulars, the question of who actually fired the opening round of the war is, in itself, no mean subject for dispute. "First shot" claims have come under a heavy crossfire of historical argument. In fact, some will contend that the war didn't begin at Fort Sumter at all.*

At some time on April 11, 1861, it occurred to Capt. George S. James that he should send for a physician. He was about to start a war the next morning and he thought it might be well to have a doctor on hand.

The captain commanded two Confederate batteries of 10-inch mortars emplaced amid the sand dunes of James

*Later included in: Ashley Halsey, Jr., *Who Fired the First Shot?* (Greenwich, Conn.: Fawcett Publications, Inc., Crest Book d671, 1963), pp. 27-36.

Island at Fort Johnson, facing Fort Sumter in Charleston harbor. The doctor who responded to his call, although not needed professionally as it turned out, had a wonderful opportunity to become the star witness in what is now a major historical controversy: Who actually fired the first shot of the Civil War?

With the arrival of the war centennial, there are almost as many nominees for that notable role as there are be-whiskered characters in Cuba. They range from an elderly man to a very small girl. Let us consider the likeliest in order.

Captain James realized that his position was the logical one to fire first, because it was a point of departure and return for Confederate emissaries making an eleventh-hour attempt to negotiate a peaceful surrender at Fort Sumter. James knew that their return without surrender terms would mean war.

The captain, a veteran of the Mexican War of 1846-48, had two good lieutenants, both fresh from West Point. He posted them carefully at the mortars. There had been premature or accidental shots from the batteries surrounding Sumter. James wanted no mistake about his.

Lt. Wade Hampton Gibbes, a newlywed who had served briefly as a United States cavalry lieutenant after graduation from the Military Academy the previous June, commanded at one mortar emplacement. Lt. Henry S. Farley, the first Southern cadet to walk out of West Point without waiting to be graduated, commanded the other. Both were young South Carolinians willing, if not eager, to begin a war in their own back yard.

Both lieutenants later claimed the crepe-draped distinction of having fired the first shot. As a witness, the physician, Dr. Robert Lebby, proved somewhat less than conclusive. He was talking with another doctor, the garrison surgeon, who had been away but returned just in time. Both medical men saw Farley holding the lanyard which set off his mortar and are "of the opinion" that he fired first. In the leisurely way of newspapers of the day, *The Charleston Mercury* got around to this bit of news a week later. "We are informed," it said, "that Lieut. H. S. Farley of Captain James's company had the honor of firing the alarm or first gun of the battle on Friday last."

Whoever informed *The Mercury*, it was not Lt. Wade Hampton Gibbes. That officer stated, "The first shell was fired by Captain James's battery, and, incidentally, by me as his first lieutenant." Gibbes outranked Farley, who was a second lieutenant. In the protocol of starting a war, he held an advantage. He was explicit: "My orders were to fire a shell, to burst high up in the air, as a signal to commence the general bombardment." A shell did exactly that, exploding directly above Fort Sumter. Nearly a dozen Confederate batteries on islands around the fort then opened up full blast at ranges of 1,210 to 2,425 yards.

From a battery at the northern end of Morris Island, near the harbor entrance, there soon resounded another claim to having fired the first shot of the war. Fiery old Virginian Edmund Ruffin served there as a volunteer in the Palmetto Guards. Ruffin turned to war with a distinguished record as an agriculturist. By the experimental use of marl, he had saved thousands of acres of "sour" land. Now he was determined to save his land in another sense.

Ruffin stepped forward, yanked the lanyard of an enormous siege cannon weighing nearly five tons and shouted exuberantly that he had scored the first hit on Fort Sumter, three quarters of a mile away. For a man of sixty-seven, early on a dark and foggy morning, he demonstrated remarkable eyesight. More remarkable still, the feat was confirmed by a strange source—the senior captain of the Federal garrison in Sumter. This was Abner Doubleday, a mustachioed Yankee who fired the first return shot from the fort. Doubleday, who ended the war as a major general and was acclaimed, inaccurately, as the inventor of baseball, reminisced after the conflict:

"Edmund Ruffin of Virginia is usually credited with opening the attack by firing the first gun from the iron-clad battery on Morris Island. The ball from that gun struck the wall of the magazine where I was lying, penetrated the masonry and burst very near my head."

Doubleday surely had ample reason to remember a shell which struck that close to him. But how he could tell, through a solid brick wall on a foggy morning, who fired the shot from behind a distant battlement is one of those little mysteries which make Civil War stories so intriguing. The mystery is heightened by the fact that the Confederates discharged forty-seven cannon and mortars in rapid order after the opening shot. All together, they fired between 3,000 and 4,000 shells at the fort. Some 2,500 registered hits. For Doubleday to single out and glorify the shot that almost killed him as "the first shot of the war" somehow smacks of egotism.

Moreover, Ruffin, by his own statement in writing, was not in the "iron-clad battery" at all, although Doubleday, contemporary Charleston newspapers and other supposedly authoritative sources said that he was. Ruffin's unit, the Palmetto Guards, manned both the "Iron Battery"—so called because the battlement in front of it was iron-plated—and the "Point Battery" at the Cummings Point extremity of Morris Island. The old man, in a letter written only a week later, referred to "the Point Battery in which I was engaged."

Ruffin, at any rate, went triumphantly home to Virginia and his 200 slaves soon after Sumter yielded. He felt exhilarated. His beloved South had rebuffed the North without the loss of a single life on either side. Despite the terrific bombardment, the massive brick fort amply protected its little garrison. Only four men were wounded. Ironically, one accidental fatality occurred later when a

56

fort cannon, firing a salute to the Stars and Stripes before the garrison marched out, went off prematurely. It killed a Federal gunner instantly and wounded five others.

Ruffin subsequently wrote a polite "thank you" note to his host of April the twelfth and thirteenth, the commanding officer of the Palmetto Guards, expressing appreciation for the use of his cannon. He also established himself as one of the first souvenir hunters of the Civil War. He asked his comrades to recover a Federal shell which he had seen bury itself in the sand near the Point Battery, and express it to him at Petersburg, Virginia, "as a memento of the occasion."

Before the war ended, Ruffin and his compatriots found more than enough Federal shells coming their way unsolicited. Doggedly shouldering his musket, the old planter made brief, cheer-raising appearances at the Battle of First Manassas or Bull Run, and on return trips to the defenses around Charleston. By 1863 he was dodging from his plantations to avoid Federal troops. As the South went down, the old man sank with it. Two months after Appomattox, he shot and killed himself rather than live "conquered" under "Yankee rule."

Like Ruffin, the lieutenants of the mortar batteries, Gibbes and Farley, survived four years of conflict. Gibbes remained in the artillery, becoming a major. He suffered a grave wound in the Battle of the Crater at Petersburg. In postwar life he became a banker, machinery dealer and senior warden of Trinity Episcopal Church at Columbia, South Carolina. Farley shifted to the cavalry and eventually became a lieutenant colonel. After the war, he conducted a military academy at Ossining, New York. A daughter of his married the late United States Senator E. D. Smith of South Carolina, and a grandson, Farley Smith of Sumter, now heads the anti-integration South Carolina Citizens Councils.

Among those publicized in 1861 as rivals of the three

warlike Southerners for the distinction of starting the war was, fantastically, a small girl who happened to have the Czarina of Russia as a godmother. The child, daughter of Francis W. Pickens of South Carolina and his beautiful Texan wife, was born in St. Petersburg in 1859 while her father was United States Ambassador to Russia. Amid much pomp, she was christened Frances Eugenia Olga Neva Pickens. The Czar thereupon nicknamed her Douschka, or "little darling," a name borne today by her granddaughter.

Pickens soon returned to South Carolina and became governor. To be at the center of crisis in 1861, he moved with his family from the state capital at Columbia to temporary quarters in the Charleston Hotel. The more lurid section of the Northern press described in detail how tiny Douschka fired the opening gun of the war while held in the arms of the Confederate commander, Gen. P. G. T. Beauregard. The fanciful story was presented as evidence of the wanton attitude of the South toward bloodshed. Not a single fact can be found to support it. When the war began, little Douschka apparently was asleep at the hotel miles away. She was, after all, only about two. Nor was Beauregard present in the batteries that opened on Sumter. The nearest thing to a Confederate kiddy act occurred at the Iron Battery, where thirteen-year-old Paul B. Lalane, who cleverly picked the occasion to visit an elder brother in the service, was permitted to fire several shells at Sumter.

With the Civil War centennial, all "first shot" claims have come under a heavy crossfire of historical argument. In some places local chroniclers or Chamber of Commerce trumpeters even contend that the war didn't begin at Fort Sumter at all. These place the locale in Florida, Mississippi and Arkansas. Each involves a "first shot" fired before the bombardment of Sumter. Here is the sequence:

At Pensacola, Florida, January 8, 1861, United States troops in old Fort Barrancas, commanded by Lt. Adam J. Slemmer, drove off with a volley of musketry twenty shadowy figures. Presumably the twenty were state troops scouting to see if the fort was garrisoned. The shots were, without doubt, the first discharged in support of the Union.

The next day at Charleston, salvos from a harbor battery turned back the merchant steamship *Star of the West*, out of New York for Charleston with supplies for Fort Sumter. Cadets of the South Carolina Military Academy, now The Citadel, manned the guns. These were the first shots fired at the United States flag.

Within a week rebel shells brought another United States craft to a halt at Vicksburg, Mississippi. Capt. J. F. Kerr's battery from Jackson fired two shots in front of a paddle-wheeler bound from Pittsburgh to New Orleans. Militiamen then searched the ship for supplies for the United States forts around New Orleans, found none and let her go.

In a third incident involving supplies for forts, early in April, the Jefferson Guards of Pine Bluff, Arkansas, rallied at the river bank and diverted a supply transport bound up the Arkansas to Fort Smith. One musket bullet across the bows apparently did the trick. The "sovereign" State of Arkansas then confiscated the military material on board.

The Charleston harbor defenses meanwhile fired on the United States flag a second time. Their target was a little schooner loaded with New England ice for Savannah. The craft blundered up the channel in a fog, without any way of explaining her appearance there. When the guns began to boom, she flew out again like a frightened sparrow.

None of these almost comic performances with artillery scratched a single person, much less set off a gigantic

59

conflict. So the claims of Gibbes, Farley and Ruffin—take your pick—would appear to head the list. Or do they?

When it comes to historical assertions, the Civil War centennial is a "shooting war" in itself. Any statement raised above the parapets whether by Civil War buffs or innocent bystanders, is subject to being drilled full of Minié holes from one direction or another. Here, coming from one of their contemporaries, is a bombshell for Gibbes and Farley.

It fell to Capt. (later Lt. Gen.) Stephen D. Lee, as an aide to the commanding general, P. G. T. Beauregard, to break off the negotiations with Fort Sumter and transmit personally to Captain James the order to open fire. In a statement years later, Lee relates how James in his courtly way invited Roger Pryor, a hotheaded Virginia lawyer and newspaperman who was a sort of younger version of Ruffin, to fire the opening shot. As Lee recalled it, James turned to Pryor and said, "You are the only man to whom I would give up the honor of firing the first gun of the war." Pryor could not bring himself to bear the awesome responsibility. Huskily he declined. At that, Lee says flatly, "Captain James would allow no one else but *himself* to fire the gun."

Lee, however, undermined his own testimony. En route back to Charleston and headquarters, he had his boatmen row him about 800 yards away, where he could witness the effect of the shelling. Obviously he was not at hand to see who first jerked the lanyard. Yet he maintained to the end that it was James.

General Beauregard stated after the war in *Military Operations,* Chapter IV, Page 42: "From Fort Johnson's mortar battery at 4.30 A.M. issued the first shot of the war. It was fired not by Mr. Ruffin of Virginia, as has been erroneously supposed, but by Captain George S. James of South Carolina."

Here was the commanding general's word for it, but the

general, like his aide, Stephen D. Lee, was not present in person to see for himself. Another of his aides, Lieut. Edward H. Barnwell, testified that the first shell soared from "*James' east or beach battery*." This raised a point. The general referred to one battery; the lieutenant implied there were two under command of James. And indeed there were, adding to the historical confusion.

A precise account in after years from Dr. W. H. Prioleau (pronounced pray-low), of Charleston, surgeon of the post, who was absent when Captain James summoned Dr. Lebby but who returned before the guns spoke, confirms that the mortars under James were divided into two batteries or sections.

"On the morning of April 12, 1861," Dr. Prioleau stated, "as soon as orders were received to open fire on Fort Sumter, we repaired to our posts, and 25 or 30 minutes after 4 A.M., by my watch, which I held open in my hand at the time, the first gun was fired, this being the righthand mortar in the *battery on the beach*. I cannot recall who pulled the lanyard, but the gun was directly in charge of Lieut. Henry S. Farley, who, as well as I can recollect, righted the gun, Captain James giving the order to fire."

Dr. Lebby amplified on this and added his own observations in a paper written in 1893 and published in 1911 in the *South Carolina Historical Magazine*. In it, Lebby, a native, resident and practicing physician of James Island, explained that, "having been a college acquaintance of Captain James, (I) was invited by him the previous day, April 11, to be on hand if anything transpired to require my services."

Lebby then bore out his colleague's reference to two batteries. These he identified as "one directly west of Fort Sumter known as the east or beach battery and one northwest of that on a hill near quarantine known as the west or hill battery.

"I was," he continued, "on a bridge that connected the beach and the hill, where I could see the fire of either battery, and at 4:30 A.M. a shell was fired from the east or beach battery commanded by Captain James.

"The second report heard was the blowing up of Greer's house, contiguous to the hill battery commanded by Lieut. W. H. Gibbes, and the second shell was fired from this battery under Lieutenant Gibbes. The firing then became general around the harbor batteries bearing on Fort Sumter. . . .

(The Greer house mentioned as being blown up in the "second report" of the war was a private home which masked the hill battery and therefore was deliberately destroyed. Similar steps were taken on the other side of the harbor, on Sullivan's Island, where the Confederates had erected several batteries, unknown to the defenders of Fort Sumter, behind buildings.)

"As to the question of who pulled the lanyard . . . certain it is that either James or Farley fired it, but as Captain James *gave the order* to fire, it must have been Farley, as James would never have given *himself* the order to fire."

Not content with this deduction, Dr. Lebby wrote to Colonel Farley, then at Mount Pleasant Military Academy on the Hudson River. Farley's reply is incorporated in the doctor's published account.

"The circumstances attending the firing of the first gun at Sumter are quite fresh in my memory," the aging colonel said stoutly. "Captain James stood on my right, watch in hand, and at the designated moment gave me the order to fire. *I pulled the lanyard,* having already carefully inserted a friction tube, and discharged a 13-inch mortar . . . which was at the right of the battery."

All in all, it would appear that Farley's claim was borne out by two physicians and the circumstantial testimony of General Beauregard and two of his aides. It did not, however, silence Gibbes' steadfast statement that his mortar got off the first shot. Nor did it faze the embattled Ruffin in his vaunting at the time.

Much of Ruffin's fame derives from an ambiguous newspaper report. This, a camouflage of facts with words, says that the venerable Virginian "fired the first shot at Fort Sumter from the Iron Battery on Morris Island." All it meant, taken in context, was that he began one battery's part in the bombardment.

To aggravate matters, I, in writing this, must remove another laurel from the grim old secessionist's war record. No matter how close his cannon ball shaved past Abner Doubleday's head, technically it was *not* the first shell to strike Sumter. The first shot ever landed on the fort hit it much earlier—March 8, 1861, to be exact.

It was during the "cold war" between the Federal Government and the seceding states. Southern artillerymen at Charleston continually tested their guns, usually taking care to aim well clear of the frowning fortress under the Stars and Stripes. To citizen soldiers in the Iron Battery, unaccustomed to heaving about heavy cannon, the toil of endless drills seemed pointless. One night, a twenty-three-year-old private remarked that he was "tired of this nonsense—there will be some fun in the morning."

Shortly after dawn, when the battery went through all the empty motions of firing, an eight-inch columbiad suddenly roared out while aimed at the fort. The solid shot screamed across the water at Sumter. It struck, according to one version, just to the left of the sally port or main gate. The garrison manned its guns—this is a matter of official record—and prepared to reply to further shelling. Instead, the Iron Battery commander rushed over in a small boat under a truce flag to apologize for "the accidental shot."

The shot was no accident. I can say that with certainty, for the man who loaded the gun during the night was my grandfather, E. L. Halsey of Charleston. Grandfather was not the patient type. The explosive gesture seemed entirely representative of his feelings. If action was what he wanted, he soon got it. Transferring from harbor defenses to horse artillery, he became first lieutenant and then captain of a battery which fought in 143 battles and skirmishes from start to finish. Of the unit's original 147 men, only twenty-three answered the final muster. At the surrender they cried as they kissed their cannon good-by. Grandfather broke his saber and kept his revolver.

After the war, with much of the South burned to the ground, grandfather went into the lumber business. He made a small fortune, married a golden-haired young lady eleven years his junior and fathered seven sons and five daughters. He lived out his days totally unreconstructed. My father, as a boy, erected a small United States flag on a pole in the garden one Christmas Day. My grandfather, wordless with anger, got out his revolver, chopped down the pole with three precisely placed bullets and said, "I do not want to see that flag on my premises ever again!" He didn't.

Never, however, did he make any public statement about his attempt to start the Civil War a month ahead of time with the shot that hit Sumter in March. Possibly, having become a veteran soldier, he realized what a breach of discipline his prank represented. When an account of it was published many years ago, my Uncle LeRoy, who lives at Stone Mountain, near Atlanta, recalls that grandfather "was not pleased at it."

As for deciding who actually fired the opening round, Samuel G. Stoney, Charleston's bearded historian, once settled the question facetiously: "Many people believe 'The War' was so big that it was entitled to more than one opening shot."

The article was 3,500 words long. Divide the number of minutes you spent reading it into 3,500, and you will have your reading rate in words per minute. Your prereading should have consumed no more than two minutes. When you have calculated your words per minute, answer the following questions to test your comprehension.

1—Which of the following men is the most likely candidate for the honor of firing the first shot at Sumter?
    a. Gibbes
    b. Farley
    c. Ruffin
    d. James

2—The mortar battery from which the shot was fired was the
    a. north battery
    b. east battery
    c. south battery
    d. west battery

3—Gibbes commanded the
    a. hill battery
    b. beach battery
    c. lake battery
    d. bridge battery

4—Abner Doubleday corroborated the story of
    a. Gibbes
    b. Farley
    c. Ruffin
    d. James

5—Which of the following did Dr. Prioleau see pull the lanyard?
   a. James
   b. Farley
   c. Gibbes
   d. He didn't see anyone pull it.

6—Stephen D. Lee was
   a. a southern general in command of the fort
   b. a captain in charge of a mortar battery
   c. a second lieutenant under Gibbes
   d. an aide to General Beauregard

7—Dr. Lebby was at
   a. Fort Sumter
   b. Fort Johnson
   c. between the two mortar batteries when the firing occurred
   d. b and c

8—The firing on Fort Sumter began at
   a. 3:30 a.m.
   b. 4:00 a.m.
   c. 4:30 a.m.
   d. 5:00 a.m.

9—In civilian life, Ruffin was
   a. an engineer
   b. an agriculturist
   c. a ballistics expert
   d. a banker

10—Farley
   a. was the first southern cadet to leave West Point without graduating when hostilities broke out
   b. later became a banker
   c. opened a military academy after the war.
   d. a and c

(*Answers on p. 170*)

Day III

Phrase Reading Exercise #3

But it seemed fated   that Feliu's waif   should
never be identified;—diligent inquiry   and printed
announcements   alike proved fruitless.   Sea
and sand   had either hidden   or effaced   all
the records   of the little world   they had en-
gulfed: the annihilation   of whole families,
the extinction   of races, had,   in more than
one instance   rendered vain   all efforts   to
recognize   the dead.   It required   the
subtle perception   of long intimacy   to name
remains   tumefied and discolored   by corrup-
tion and exposure,   mangled and gnawed   by
fishes,   by reptiles,   and by birds.   And
sometimes   all who had loved   the lost
were themselves   among the missing.   The full
roll-call   of names   could never be made out
—extraordinary mistakes   were committed.   Men
whom the world   deemed dead   and buried
came back, like ghosts,   —to read   their own
epitaphs.*

*Lafcadio Hearn, *op. cit.*, p. 82

67

Indenting Exercise #3

Even to-day, in these Creole islands, the advent of the steamer is the great event of the week. There are no telegraph lines, no telephones: the mail-packet is the only trustworthy medium of communication with the outer world, bringing friends, news, letters. The magic of steam has placed New Orleans nearer to New York than to the Timbaliers, nearer to Washington than to Wine Island, nearer to Chicago than to Barataria Bay. And even during the deepest sleep of waves and winds there will come betimes to sojourners in this unfamiliar archipelago a feeling of lonesomeness that is a fear, a feeling of isolation from the world of men,—totally unlike that sense of solitude which haunts one in the silence of mountain-heights, or amid the eternal tumult of lofty granitic coasts: a sense of helpless insecurity. The land seems but an undulation of the sea-bed: its highest ridges do not rise more than the height of a man above the salines on either side;—the salines themselves lie almost level with the level of the floodtides;—the tides are variable, treacherous, mysterious.*

Eye-Swing Exercise #2

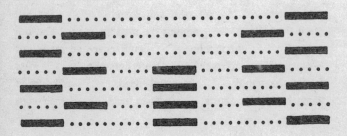

*Lafcadio Hearn, *op. cit.,* p. 39

Visualizing and Direction-Following

Whether you are building a boat, following a recipe, or trying to understand a scientific experiment, you must be able to *follow directions* and *visualize* the final product. This is a skill that comes more easily to some than to others; it will depend on the type of thinking to which you are accustomed. But it is a skill that needs development to round out your reading approach. Read the following selection, then *draw* what it represents.

Visualizing and Direction-Following Exercise #1

Deal one card face up, then six face down in the same row toward the right. Deal one face up on the card just to the right of the first face up, then add another face down on each card to the right. Continue in the same manner, dealing one less card each round, turning the first face up, the rest face down.*

Draw the result:

*Richard L. Frey, *According to Hoyle* (Greenwich, Conn.: Fawcett Publications, Inc., Crest Book R617, 1957), p. 192.

Question: Give an example of the feedback mechanism.

Cybernetics is a new science that treats *message* as a control factor. Whenever a message is transmitted, the sender exercises a certain amount of control over the receiver; the receiver, in turn, responds with *feedback,* or a response to the message that conditions subsequent messages. For example, Mr. A asks Mr. B to give him more room on a car seat (message); Mr. B acts as though he doesn't hear (feedback); Mr. A repeats his message louder (message in response to feedback), etc., etc. Similarly, a plumber turning a screwdriver may be considered as transmitting a message to the screw. When the screw refuses to turn, he receives feedback, and either applies more pressure or stops trying to turn it.

Messages and feedback may exist between persons and other persons, persons and machines, or machines and other machines. The more trite the message, the less control it exercises.

How to Read a Book
(Non-Fiction)

To begin with, there are three general types of non-fiction books: those that attempt to survey an entire field (most textbooks fall into this category); those with a single thesis or point to make (for instance, books on the contemporary political situation); and, finally, those in chronicle form (most history and biography fall into this category). We will consider the first two types in this chapter and save the latter type for tomorrow's lesson.

No matter what type of non-fiction book you are presently reading (aside from this one), if you are having any trouble it is no doubt because you have lost the *point of view* of the book. Every book, no matter how large, must have some binding factor to make it a unified whole. This is its point of view; once you find it, you will have no trouble. Consider for a moment a fairly lengthy book: it will probably contain 200,000 words. If you had an average 200-250 wpm reading rate, and could afford to spend three or four hours a week on the book, it would take you about a month and a half to finish it. No wonder you had trouble!

There are two steps you can take to solve your problem. First of all (as you have probably realized already), you have to improve your general approach to the page. By pre-reading each chapter and by utilizing the techniques of phrase reading, you will increase your reading rate to the point where the time spent reading will be more commensurate with the information actually contained in the book. Secondly, by using all the comprehension aids which publishers provide but most readers

71

ignore, you will be able to see the book's point of view, follow its main idea, and keep yourself from getting lost or "bogged down" over the course of a fairly long work. This second point will be our primary consideration in this chapter.

When you first choose a book, place it in a context. Take a book off your shelf now, preferably one that you haven't read. What is the title and who is the author? Do you know anything about the author, his interests, his opinions, any recurring themes in his work? If you do, how do you relate your knowledge of this author to the title and the subject of this particular book? What do you expect him to discuss?

Read the publisher's blurb on the book jacket. It will be highly laudatory, of course, but don't take the publisher's word as to the book's merit; rather, read the blurb to find some clues to what the book says. What is the problem being discussed? What are the author's solutions to it?

Next, turn to the prefatory material—the foreword, preface, and introduction. Again, read these to try to pin down the thesis of the book. Very often, if the book seems to be an important one in its field, the introduction will be written by an eminent critic, describing the book's contribution to its subject and usually summarizing the book's contents. It goes without saying that you should read this section very carefully.

The table of contents is next on your list. If you will recall, when you pre-read essays, you read the first sentence of each paragraph because that is likely to be the topic sentence. The topic sentence of a paragraph states in general terms the main idea of the rest of the paragraph. Much the same situation holds true in a book—except that there are *topic chapters* rather than topic sentences. The first chapter of a book, for instance, may state a concept in general terms, while the next five chapters will develop that concept in greater detail. Then there will be another topic chapter, followed by several more specific chapters, and so on. Quite often, the first chapter will serve as an introduction to the book, and the last chapter will conclude the work, or sum up the author's findings (just as the essay contains an introductory and concluding paragraph). Read the table of contents very carefully, then try to pick out the introductory, concluding and topic chapters. Don't just glance over it; really spend some time trying to read into it, to integrate these chapter titles into the understanding of the book which you have already gleaned from the publisher's material. If there seems to be a tricky chapter title, the meaning of which is not readily clear to you, dip into the chapter itself for a minute or two. Read the first and last paragraphs of the chapter, until the meaning of the title becomes clear. After you have picked out the important chapters, pre-read each one of them—very rapidly, of course; don't begin to get too involved in them just yet.

Finally, take a very brief look at the index, to get a more complete idea of what the book contains.

If you have followed all the steps, you should have a fairly good idea by this time as to what the book is about. In other words, you have found its scope, you know what topic is under consideration, how it is approached, and by pre-reading the concluding chapters, how the author finally resolves it. Your reading, then, should be no problem at all. You know right where you stand on each page of the book; you know what the author is discussing before you even start. You have found the book's point of view. Now you will not get lost or "bogged down."

This approach holds true for the first two types of books mentioned at the beginning of this chapter: the book with a single thesis, and the book that surveys a field. For the thesis-type book, it is obviously the thesis and the author's treatment of it that you look for as you pre-read. In the survey-type book, it is the structure of and approach to the field that you want. For example, assume you have chosen a book on biology. Before you begin to study individual chapters, try to understand the field as a whole. What does the "science of life" encompass? Can you perceive the book's progression from the simplest unicellular forms of life up to the most complex, man himself? What are the great divisions of living creatures? In other words, find out what the book deals with in general terms before you start worrying about details.

The third type of book mentioned in the beginning of today's chapter was the chronicle-type, i.e., history or biography. While the approach to this kind of writing is somewhat similar to the approach to the other types, it is also different enough to warrant a separate discussion in tomorrow's lesson.

Day IV

Key-Word Reading Exercise #2

On January 3, 1781, he was at Matoax with his mother, who only five days before had been confined. Suddenly it was said that the British were coming. They soon appeared, under the command of Brigadier-General Benedict Arnold, and scared Virginia from Yorktown to the mountains. They hunted the Governor like a tired fox, and ran him out of his famous mountain fastness at Monticello, breaking up his government and mortifying him, until Mr. Jefferson at last refused to reassume the office, and passed his trust over to a stronger hand. St. George Tucker at Matoax thought it time to seek safer quarters, and hurried his wife, with her little baby, afterwards the well-known Judge Henry St. George Tucker, away to Bizarre, ninety miles up the Appomattox.*

Here is what you should have:

　　　　　　　1781,　　　　　Matoax with　　　mother,
　　five days before　　　　　　confined.
　　　　　　　British　　　coming.　　　soon appeared,
peared,　　　　command　　　　　　　Benedict Arnold,　　scared Virginia
　　　　　　　hunted　　　Governor
　　　　out　　　　　　　mountain　　　Monticello, breaking up　　government　　mortifying
　　Mr. Jefferson　　　refused　reassume　　office,
　　passed　　trust　　to　stronger　　St George
Tucker　　　　　　　time　　seek safer
　　hurried　　wife,　　　　　　baby, afterwards
　　　　Judge Henry St. George Tucker,　　　Bizarre, ninety miles　　　Appomattox.

*Henry Adams *op. cit.,* p. 21

Sentence Correction

The good reader is so aware of the logic of language, that he quickly picks up patterns of thought as he reads and can usually anticipate the words of the author long before he comes to them. The following exercises are designed to increase this skill, to develop fluency in spotting thought patterns. One word in each of the selections is *illogical*. You are to find it and replace it with the logical one.

Sentence Correction Exercise #1

Find the illogical word in each sentence and replace it with the logical one.

1. It's nothing to get excited about; it's a very extraordinary occurrence.

2. I refuse to eat at a table with little children. No matter how charming they may be, I always find their table manners very endearing.

3. Everyone thought the atom was perfectly destructible —until the cyclotron came along and changed everything by splitting an atom.

4. The more harebrained schemes there are to disprove Shakespeare's authorship of the plays generally attributed to him, the more implausible it actually becomes that he was the author.

5. With the utmost care and imprecision, he removed the rust spots from the mainspring of the watch, until it was working perfectly again.

(*Answers on p. 170*)

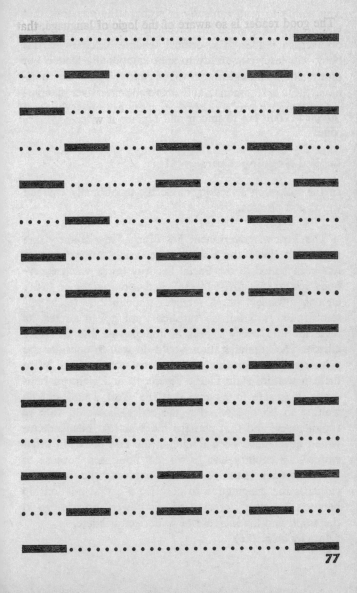

Critical Reading

The ability to read *critically* is perhaps the one trait that will always distinguish the excellent reader from the poor or average reader. The critical reading exercises in this book will test your ability to spot emotionally loaded but essentially meaningless or vague words (e.g., big business, the workingman), and also spot the flaws in arguments. Don't try to rush through these exercises; do them carefully.

Critical Reading Exercise #1

In the following selection, circle the emotionally charged words and phrases.

The Federal government has dragged the country one more step down the road to socialism. A new proviso has been added to the Social Security laws, which everybody has to pay for, as usual, and some might be lucky enough to collect on. It seems as though the present administration will not be satisfied until it can stretch its tentacles into every aspect of the private life of every citizen. The administration would do well to consider the principles on which this great country was founded. Were there a welfare state in the seventeen and eighteen hundreds, it is safe to assume that the West would still be waiting to be opened, that the railroads would still be rudimentary, and that perhaps the War for Independence would never have been fought in the first place. In other words, this country has grown and flourished because of the individual initiative of its populace, and it hardly stretches the imagination to perceive a causal relationship between the steady erosion of our power and prestige in the world and the increase of welfarism at home.

(Answers on p. 171)

Pre-read and read the following selection, timing yourself as you read. When you finish, divide the number of minutes it took you into 875 words to obtain your words per minute score, and answer the questions on the selection.

THE WIZARD OF CHITENANGO

By James Thurber

I first read *The Wizard of Oz* as a boy of ten. Recently, I chanced to see what Oz revisited was like. I was amazed and disturbed to discover that there are now thirty-nine different books about Oz. Since the first was published more than 60 years ago, many millions of copies of Oz books have been sold. The thing is obviously a major phenomenon in the wonderful land of books. In revisiting Oz, I began my research not by rereading the Oz book I loved as a child (and still do, I was happy to find out later) but with an inquiry into the life and nature of the man who wrote the first fourteen of the series, Mr. L. Frank Baum.

Lyman Frank Baum was born in Chitenango, New York, in 1856. When he was about ten he became enamoured of (if also a little horrified and disgusted by) the tales of the Grimm brothers and of Andersen, and he determined that when he grew up he would write fairy tales with a difference. There would be, in the first place, "no love and marriage in them." Furthermore, he wanted to get away from the "European background" and write tales about fairies in America (he chose Kansas as the jumping off place for the Oz books, although he was educated in Syracuse, lived most of his life in Chicago, and spent his last years in Hollywood, where he died in 1919, aged 63). There was also another significant change that he wanted to make in the old fairy tales. Let me quote from his own foreword to *The Wizard of Oz:* "... the time has now come for a series of newer 'wonder tales' in which the stereotyped genie, dwarf and fairy are eliminated, together with all the horrible and bloodcurdling incidents devised by their authors to point a fearsome moral. ... *The Wizard of Oz* aspires to be a modernized fairy tale in which the wonderment and joy are retained, and the heartaches and nightmares left out." I am glad that, in spite of this high determination, Mr. Baum failed to keep them out. Children love a lot of nightmare and at least a little heartache in their books. And they get them in the Oz books. I know that I went through excruciatingly lovely nightmares and heartaches when the Scarecrow lost his straw, when the Tin Woodman was taken apart, when the Saw-Horse broke his wooden leg (it hurt for me, even if it didn't for Mr. Baum).

But let me return for a moment to the story of his writings. In his late twenties he wrote two plays, *The Maid of Arran* and *The Queen of Killarney*. Under the name of Schuyler Stanton, he also wrote three novels. (I could not learn their titles.) In all, he wrote about fifty books, most of them for children. He was forty-three in 1899 when he did *The Wizard of Oz,* which to him was just another (the twentieth or so) book for children. It sold better than anything he had ever written. The next year he wrote a thing called *Dot and Tot in Merryland.* But his readers wanted more about Oz. He began to get letters from them by the thousands, and he was not exactly pleased that Oz was the land they loved the best. He ignored the popular demand for four years, meanwhile writing a book called *Baum's American Fairy Tales,* subtitled "Stories of Astonishing Adventures of American Boys and Girls with the Fairies of Their Native Land." He must have been hurt by its cold reception. Here he was, nearly fifty, trying to be what he had always fondly wanted to be, an American Andersen, an American Grimm, and all the while American children—and their parents—would have none of it, but screamed for more about Oz. His American fairy tales, I am sorry to tell you, are not good fairy tales. The scene of the first one is the attic of a house "on Prairie Avenue, in Chicago." It never leaves there for any wondrous, faraway realm. Baum apparently never entirely understood that fatal flaw in his essential ambition, but he understood it a little. He did another collection of unconnected stories, but this time he placed them, not in Illinois but in Mo. *The Magical Monarch of Mo* is not much better than the American tales; but at least one story in it, *The Strange Adventures of the King's Head,* is a fine, fantastic fairy tale. The others are just so-so. On went L. Frank Baum, grimly, into the short tales making up *The Enchanted Island of Yew;* but the girls and boys were not interested. Finally, after four years and ten thousand letters from youngsters, he wrote *The Land of Oz.* He was back where they wanted him.

I haven't space to go into even half of the Oz books, nor do I want to. The first two, "The Wizard" and "The Land," are far and away the best. Baum wrote "The Wizard," I am told, simply as a *tour de force* to see if he could animate, and make real, creatures never alive before on sea or land. He succeeded, eminently, with the Scarecrow and the Tin Woodman, and he went on to succeed again in the second book with Jack Pumpkinhead, the Saw-Horse and the Woggle Bug. After that I do not think he was ever really successful. Admittedly he didn't want to keep doing Oz books. (He wanted to get back to those American Tales.) In the next six years he wrote only two, and at the end of the second of these he put a tired, awkward note explaining that Oz was somehow forever cut off from communication with this world.

What a heartache and a nightmare that announcement was to the children of America! But of course they didn't fall for his clumsy device: they knew he was a great wizard and could get back to Oz if he wanted to, and they made him get back. From 1910 until he died in 1919, he resignedly wrote an Oz book every year. He had no more chance of cutting off Oz from communication with our world than Conan Doyle had when he tried to end the Sherlock Holmes stories by pushing the great detective off a cliff during a fight with Professor Moriarty.*

Now test yourself:

1. Mr. Thurber began his revisit to Oz by
    a. rereading *The Wizard of Oz*.
    b. finding out more about the wizard of Chitenango.
    c. inquiring into the life and nature of the author.
    d. b and c.

2. Which of the following was not a change Mr. L. Frank Baum wished to make in his "fairy tales with a difference"?
    a. Americanization of background.
    b. heartaches and nightmares are left out, while wonderment and joy remain.
    c. Love and marriage are to be regarded realistically.
    d. The stereotyped genies, dwarfs, and fairies used to point fearsome morals would be eliminated.

3. *The Wizard of Oz*
    a. was the first children's book written by Baum.
    b. sold better than any book Baum had written before.
    c. was felt by the author to be the best thing he had done to date.
    d. set up a demand for Oz books which was enthusiastically satisfied by the author.

*L. Frank Baum, *op. cit.*, pp. vii-xi

4. *Baum's American Fairy Tales*
    a. were not well received.
    b. are regarded by Thurber as Baum's finest creations.
    c. were written before the publication of his *Wizard of Oz*.
    d. b and c.
5. Which of the following is not mentioned as a setting for Baum's stories?
    a. Illinois.
    b. Kansas.
    c. Mo.
    d. California.
6. "The Wizard" and "The Land" were
    a. mentioned as the best of the Oz series.
    b. the first two books in the Oz series.
    c. written four years apart.
    d. all of the above.
7. It is mentioned that Baum's original objective in writing "The Wizard" was
    a. to make improvements in his financial affairs.
    b. to maintain his status as an American Andersen or Grimm.
    c. to see if he could make real a group of creatures never seen before on land or sea.
    d. to please his nephews and nieces.
8. One of the following creatures was not created by Baum for the Oz series
    a. Scarecrow.
    b. Jack Pumpkinhead.
    c. Tin Woodman.
    d. Gold Bug.
9. Baum's attitude toward continuing the series
    a. revealed his enthusiasm for the Oz books.
    b. was dependent upon the public's reception of the work.

    c. is revealed in his attempt to sever communication
       between the earth and Oz.

    d. is not mentioned in the article.

10. From 1910 until 1919 Frank Baum

    a. retired from writing.

    b. discontinued the Oz series.

    c. wrote an Oz book every year.

    d. cut off communication with Oz.

(*Answers on p. 171*)

Vocabulary Study #1

Following is a list of the more unusual words from the selection you have just read. You will need your dictionary to complete this exercise.

phenomenon—1. Anything that is apparent to the senses and that can be scientifically described. 2. Anything that is extremely unusual. Gr. *phainomenon* (appearing).
    What is phenomenalism and phenomenology?

enamored (Br. enamoured)—Greatly in love; charmed; captivated. L. *in* (in) and *amor* (love).
    Who would a young man's inamorata be?
    Does an amateur get paid for what he does?

stereotype—1. A printing plate cast in metal from a mold. 2. An unvarying form or pattern; fixed or conventional expression, notion, character, etc.; having no individuality. Gr. *stereos* (solid, firm, three-dimensional).
    What is stereophonic sound?

How to Read History
and Biography

The third lesson considered the best ways for you to
approach the first two general divisions of non-fiction
books—the single thesis work and the survey of a general
field. The approach in both cases was similar: make ju-
dicious use of all the help provided you by the publisher
and author—such as the table of contents, the foreword,
the preface, and the introduction—to pin down the thesis
of the book and to understand the extent of the book's
scope and the subject that is being considered; skim
through the index to get a good idea of the range of material dealt with in the book; pick out topic chapters or
main idea and transitional chapters and pre-read them;
pre-read the first and last chapters of the book as introductory and concluding chapters; in general, *understand*
what you are getting into before you plunge blindly ahead.

Your approach to works of history and biography will
be essentially the same—except for one major difference.
In the first type of book, the "thesis" work, the author
was doing his best to convey the main idea; in the second
type, the survey of a field, the author took pains to present his subject in the clearest and most logical way possible. For instance, a book on biology will start with a
consideration of life in general, then work up from a study
of the simplest, one-celled creatures to the progressively
more complex beings, culminating with a study of human
biology. Everything is clear-cut, simplified and organized.
Most of the work has been done for you; all you have to
do is cooperate with the author.

When you turn to history and biography, however, no such situation exists. History, in its simplest form, is essentially a chronicle—an account of events as they happened.

Just by following current events in your daily newspaper, you are undoubtedly aware of the fact that history is not made with the same mathematical precision with which, say, the laws of physics operate; there is too much of the human factor involved. The closer a history book comes to being an accurate day-by-day chronicle of events, the less logical it must necessarily be. This is not to say that there is no logic to history; there is. But, more often than not, *you will have to put it there*. Now the burden is on *you* to deduce the "main idea" behind a history book, to synthesize the events it recounts, to see the broad patterns that move the world: in short, to *impose* a logic upon history. As you can see, this is quite a different problem from that posed by your other kinds of reading. Let's take an historical example and see how it should be dealt with.

The Renaissance always offers a fertile field for historical discussion. To refresh your memory, let us briefly review the background and events of the period. From about the eighth century on, Europe lay under the pall of the so-called "Dark Ages." Feudalism was the order of the day; Europe was segmented into tiny robber baronies; the position of the serf was no better than that of livestock; ignorance and illiteracy were rife. The only learning and research was carried on by monks, but always inside the walls of the monastery. Then suddenly, in the fifteenth and sixteenth centuries, a great upheaval began in southern Europe and spread rapidly over the Continent and England. There was a "renaissance," a rebirth of interest in the arts and science. This led to the Age of Exploration, the Elizabethan Age, the Protestant Reformation, the Catholic Counter Reformation. At the feet of the Old World lay new lands with untold riches, just for the asking. Galileo, and then Newton, was reaching out to the stars, to learn more about the universe. Europe was suddenly on the move again, vibrant and pulsating with a new strength and vigor that would spill over into new lands and continents and carry the world inexorably into the modern age.

But the question—the big question—is, *Why?*

That is the question that only history can answer. You cannot let yourself be satisfied with learning the chronicle of the times; now you must find logic behind it, the answer to the question, Why?

There may be numerous answers, of course. For example, many feel that the germ of the Renaissance lay in the "scientific method" developed by Bacon and his successors. They can trace from this method a growing individuality, a loss of faith in the old dogmas and philosophical bromides, a throwing off of superstition, a sudden discovery of naval science, physics and mathematics, all leading to greater and greater discoveries. From the individuality that science must foster, they see the growth of an atmosphere that would permit a religious revolt, that would permit free reign of artistic expression, that, in short, would permit a phenomenon like the Renaissance. Others feel that the answer lies in the Crusades. Perhaps it is a combination of the two. But that is not our point here. Our point is that history, to be understood at all, must not be studied in terms of fragments, or isolated events—in other words, in straight chronicle form—but rather in terms of a pattern and a logic that must be imposed on the chronicle by an astute and thinking reader.

Always pre-read history, then, in order to discern the logic that lies behind it. A good way to do this is to pre-read the work three times on three different levels: once from the political point of view, looking only for those sections which deal with the politics of the times, then from the social point of view, and finally from the economic point of view. Almost all historical events will fit into at least one of these three considerations. But whatever your approach, don't let yourself get bogged down in a mass of names, dates and trivial incidents. A history book should never read like a telephone book. There is a pattern and a logic to all of history, and this is what you must look for when you read this sort of material.

Day V

Phrase Reading Exercise #4

Though   our new-made foretopman   was well
received   in the top   and on the gun decks,
    hardly here was he   that cynosure
he had previously been   among those   minor
ship's companies   of the merchant marine,
with which companies only   had he hitherto con-
sorted.

He was young;   and despite his   all but
fully developed frame,   in aspect   looked even
younger   than he really was.   This was owing
    to a lingering   adolescent expression
in the as yet smooth face,   all but feminine
in purity   of natural complexion,   but where,
    thanks to his seagoing,   the lily   was
quite suppressed   and the rose   had some ado
    visibly to flush   through the tan.*

Key-Word Reading Exercise #3

John Randolph, the embodiment of these contrasts and
peculiarities, was an eccentric type recognized and understood by Virginians. To a New England man, on the
contrary, the type was unintelligible and monstrous. The
New Englander had his own code of bad manners, and
was less tolerant than the Virginian of whatever varied
from it. As the character of Don Quixote was to Cervantes
clearly a natural and possible product of Spanish character, so to the people of Virginia John Randolph was a

*The Shorter Novels of Herman Melville (Greenwich,
Conn.: Fawcett Publications, Inc., Premier Book d105,
1960), p. 205.

representative man, with qualities exaggerated but genuine; and even these exaggerations struck a chord of
popular sympathy; his very weaknesses were caricatures
of Virginia failings; his genius was in some degree a
caricature of Virginian genius; and thus the boy grew up
to manhood, as pure a Virginian Quixote as ever an
American Cervantes could have conceived.*

Here is what you should have:

John Randolph,

                eccentric type   under-
stood by Virginians. To   New England
                       unintelligible   monstrous.
New Englander   own code   bad manners,
    less tolerant than   Virginian
        As   Don Quixote   to Cervantes
            natural   product   Spanish
        so to   Virginia   Randolph
representative   qualities exaggerated   genuine;   even   exaggerations
        sympathy;   weaknesses   caricatures
    Virginia   genius
caricature   Virginia genius;   boy grew
    manhood,   pure   Virginian Quixote

Paragraph Development Exercise #2

Rearrange the sentences† in the proper order. What is the
topic sentence of each group?

A—

1. But her loss of the fortress, even though temporary,
   served as a warning.
2. Forts were either built or reinforced along the whole
   vast line of her settlements and influence.
3. To the disgust of the colonists, England returned

*Henry Adams, *op. cit.,* p. 25
†Paul M. Angle, *op. cit.,* pp. 109, 114

Louisbourg to France when peace was made in 1748.
4. France would strengthen her hold on North America, for the next time the British might not be so lenient.

(*Answers on p. 171*)

B—

1. Human nature being what it is, conflict between the two nations was inevitable.
2. Each had a thriving world trade with many ships on the sea lanes, and each had colonial outposts in North America, the West Indies, India, and other faraway regions.
3. In the middle years of the eighteenth century, the long-standing rivalry between England and France burst into world-wide war.
4. Each, through alliances, sought to dominate Europe, or at least to prevent the other from dominating it.
5. As world powers, no other countries approached them.

(*Answers on p. 171*)

Sentence Correction Exercise #2

Find the illogical word in each sentence and replace it with the logical one.

1. A high-pressure area pushed cool Arctic air from Canada southward down the Atlantic and raised the temperatures of the whole U.S. eastern coast by several degrees.
2. Parkinson's Law, or the Law of the Rising Pyramid, presents a tongue-in-cheek formula for calculating a business's tendency toward efficiency by the needless reduplicating of jobs.
3. The speed of air travel in the jet age has so outstripped conventional forms of transportation that it sometimes takes less time to drive to the airport than it does to fly to one's ultimate destination.
4. John has a definite conception of the ideal world, definite ideas as to how it could be arrived at, a definite

program which he feels could help almost everyone in the country work up to his true potential; he's probably the last real cynic that I know.

5. The President of France left Germany yesterday after an unsuccessful state visit. Officials on both sides felt that Franco-German relations had been greatly improved by the trip, and several economic difficulties were solved.

(*Answers on p. 171*)

Skipping and Skimming Exercise #3

Question: What is the benefit of a "limited partnership" business?

The type of business chosen must conform with the personality of the individual. Individual ownership is best for those people who have the need to dominate and run things their way.

Partnership presents the advantage of sharing both the financial and the operating responsibility of the business. Both the individual and the partnership may do business under a firm name.

The limited partnership presents the added feature of having additional investors in the business who do not have the right to interfere. They are only responsible for the firm's reverses to the extent of their investment.

The corporation offers to the stockholder protection of his personal assets from each of the firm's creditors in the event of financial reverses.*

---

*Martin J. Ross, *Handbook of Everyday Law* (Greenwich, Conn.: Fawcett Publications, Inc., Crest Book R697, 1961), pp. 178-179.

How to Read a Novel

Reading a novel is a wonderful experience. Although the novel is one of the most recently developed literary forms, the whole range of human emotion, human suffering and human triumph can be found within its pages. And this is the essential point to keep in mind when you read a novel, because unless it is a failure, a novel should be an experience for the reader. When you read nonfiction, you are interested in understanding the main idea, the pith of the article, stripped of all ornamentation; but when you read a novel, you want to identify with the characters, to live with them, to try to experience everything that they experience throughout the course of the book.

Your reason for reading novels must also affect your choice of novels. You must be the judge of what you like or don't like. Dostoevski's *Brothers Karamazov*, for instance, is a classic—and justifiably so. It sounds depths of the soul that most writers could never conceive of as existing. But the fact remains, if *you* cannot identify with the three brothers, if you cannot experience what Dostoevski wants you to experience—perhaps simply because his prose style is rambling and confusing—then *Brothers Karamazov* is not for you—for the time being at least. Start with something closer to home. Never read a novel because everybody else tells you it is good. Read it because *you* think it is good. Certainly you will follow the recommendations of those whose opinions you respect, but make sure that you are the final arbiter. If Dostoevski's works do not appeal to you, try more modern novels by authors such as John Steinbeck or Ernest Hemingway, or perhaps the urbane novels of John Marquand, or even Ian Fleming mysteries. Read what you like, but the important thing is to *read*. Later on, you may return to that classic you couldn't digest before, and suddenly find it quite palatable. But whatever your choice, remember that it is *experience* that you want from your novel, vicarious experience to be sure, but all the same, experience you couldn't possibly get on your own hook—life is too short —so miss as little of it as possible.

Keeping our objectives for reading novels in mind, we must now ask, What is the reading approach that will best realize these objectives?

First of all, allow yourself time to read the novel. If your novel is any good at all, you won't want to read it in five- or ten-minute snatches. Take at least a half hour, preferably an hour or more, when you can sit down and give the book your complete attention. Then take your time to get into it. Read the first two or three chapters slowly, trying to find the mood of the novel, the atmosphere the author is creating. Get the feel of his style. Get to know the characters. What kind of people are they? How would you expect them to react in different situations? Are they people that interest you? Finally, once you have gotten your bearings in the novel, so to speak, try to *see* the action—don't just read about it. To be sure, there are some novels, like those of James Joyce, for example, in which the play of words is crucial, but they are the exception rather than the rule. Most parts of most novels attempt to paint a picture for the reader, or better yet, attempt to *suggest* a picture. Read the following passage from Thomas Hardy's *Return of the Native:* "Perhaps as many as thirty bonfires could be counted within the bounds of the district. . . . It was as if the bonfire makers were standing in some radiant upper story of the world, detached from and independent of the dark stretches below. The heath down there was now a vast abyss, and no longer a continuation of what they stood on . . . the whole black phenomenon of the heath represented Limbo, and the muttered articulations of the wind in the hollows were as complaints and petitions from the 'souls of mighty worth' suspended therein."

Hardy is painting a vivid word-picture, using broad, sweeping strokes. He is not giving you many details; he doesn't intend to. They would make his work tedious. It is logical, then, to read the novel in the same way it is written. Don't pin yourself down to each word the author uses. See the big, broad picture. In the above passage, for instance, you should see the flickering of the bonfires; you should be standing near a fire, gazing out over the heath, inhaling all of its aromas, hearing all of its sounds, seeing and listening to the other heath-dwellers around the fires with you.

Reading a novel is mostly a question of attitude and involvement, but it precludes a rigid word-by-word approach. With the proper involvement, you will find the novel almost takes on the aspect of a moving picture. You will be able to "live it" that much more easily, and you will find it goes faster, too. The proper attitude, then —looking for the pictures and sensations on the page rather than the individual words—will increase your speed and your enjoyment, and will add greatly to the riches you will discover in novels.

Day VI

Indenting Exercise #4

... Almost every evening throughout the season there had been dancing in the great hall;—there was dancing that night also. The population of the hotel had been augmented by the advent of families from other parts of the island, who found their summer cottages insecure places of shelter: there were nearly four hundred guests assembled. Perhaps it was for this reason that the entertainment had been prepared upon a grander plan than usual, that it assumed the form of a fashionable ball. And all those pleasure-seekers,—representing the wealth and beauty of the Creole parishes,—whether from Ascension or Assumption, St. Mary's or St. Landry's, Iberville or Terrebonne, whether inhabitants of the multi-colored and many-balconied Creole quarter of the quaint metropolis, or dwellers in the dreamy paradises of the Têche,—mingled joyously, knowing each other, feeling in some sort akin—whether affiliated by blood, connaturalized by caste, or simply interassociated by traditional sympathies of class sentiment and class interest. *

Sentence Correction Exercise #3

Find the illogical word in each of the following selections and replace it with a logical word.

1. Logic is not a philosophy; it is the tool of philosophy. It is the method the philosopher uses to obscure the truth.
2. Work is under way to counteract the dangerous radioactive antitoxins that result from nuclear fallout and present a grave threat to the purity of our drinking water.

*Lafcadio Hearn, *op. cit.*, p. 43

3. Except for similarities in architecture and materials, each house was very like its neighbor.
4. Even steel, tough as it is, will bend and sag under sufficient stress. The more it is tempered, of course, the more flexible it will become, although it will never attain perfect rigidity under all conditions.
5. The sharply dropping costs of television production are largely responsible for the poor quality of video entertainment: producers simply can't afford what the public wants.

(*Answers on p. 171*)

Eye-Swing Exercise #4

Pre-read and read the following selection, timing yourself as you read. When you finish, divide the number of minutes it took you into 1,300 words to obtain your words per minute score, and answer the questions on the selection.

I

A VERY little boy stood upon a heap of gravel for the honour of Rum Alley. He was throwing stones at howling urchins from Devil's Row, who were circling madly about the heap and pelting him. His infantile countenance was livid with the fury of battle. His small body was writhing in the delivery of oaths.

"Run Jimmie, run! Dey'll git yehs!" screamed a retreating Rum Alley child.

"Naw," responded Jimmie with a valiant roar, "dese mugs can't make me run."

Howls of renewed wrath went up from Devil's Row throats. Tattered gamins on the right made a furious assault on the gravel-heap. On their small convulsed faces shone the grins of true assassins. As they charged, they threw stones and cursed in shrill chorus.

The little champion of Rum Alley stumbled precipitately down the other side. His coat had been torn to shreds in a scuffle, and his hat was gone. He had bruises on twenty parts of his body, and blood was dripping from a cut in his head. His wan features looked like those of a tiny insane demon. On the ground, children from Devil's Row closed in on their antagonist. He crooked his left arm defensively about his head and fought with madness. The little boys ran to and fro, dodging, hurling stones, and swearing in barbaric trebles.

From a window of an apartment-house that uprose from amid squat ignorant stables there leaned a curious woman. Some labourers, unloading a scow at a dock at the river, paused for a moment and regarded the fight. The engineer of a passive tugboat hung lazily over a railing and watched. Over on the island a worm of yellow convicts came from the shadow of a grey ominous building and crawled slowly along the river's bank.

A stone had smashed in Jimmie's mouth. Blood was bubbling over his chin and down upon his ragged shirt. Tears made furrows on his dirt-stained cheeks. His thin legs had begun to tremble and turn weak, causing his small body to reel. His roaring curses of the first part of the fight had changed to a blasphemous chatter. In the yells of the whirling mob of Devil's Row children there were notes of joy like songs of triumphant savagery. The little boys seemed to leer gloatingly at the blood upon the other child's face.

Down the avenue came boastfully sauntering a lad of sixteen years, although the chronic sneer of an ideal manhood already sat upon his lips. His hat was tipped over his eye with an air of challenge. Between his teeth a cigar-stump was tilted at the angle of defiance. He walked with a certain swing of the shoulders which appalled the timid. He glanced over into the vacant lot in which the little raving boys from Devil's Row seethed about the shrieking and tearful child from Rum Alley.

"Gee!" he murmured with interest, "a scrap. Gee!" He strode over to the cursing circle, swinging his shoulders in a manner which denoted that he held victory in his fists. He approached at the back of one of the most deeply engaged of the Devil's Row children. "Ah, what d' hell," he said, and smote the deeply engaged one on the back of the head.

The little boy fell to the ground and gave a tremendous howl. He scrambled to his feet, and perceiving, evidently, the size of his assailant, ran quickly off, shouting alarms. The entire Devil's Row party followed him. They came to a stand a short distance away and yelled taunting oaths at the boy with the chronic sneer.

The latter, momentarily, paid no attention to them. "What's wrong wi'che, Jimmie?" he asked of the small champion.

Jimmie wiped his blood-wet features with his sleeve. "Well, it was dis way, Pete, see? I was goin' teh lick dat Riley kid, an' dey all pitched on me."

Some Rum Alley children now came forward. The party stood for a moment exchanging vainglorious remarks with Devil's Row. A few stones were thrown at long distances, and words of challenge passed between small warriors. Then the Rum Alley contingent turned slowly in the direction of their home street. They began to give, each to each, distorted versions of the fight. Causes of retreat in particular cases were magnified. Blows dealt in the fight were enlarged to catapultian power, and stones thrown were alleged to have hurtled with infinite accuracy. Valour grew strong again, and the little boys began to brag with great spirit. "Ah, we blokies kin lick d' hull damn Row," said a child, swaggering.

Little Jimmie was trying to stanch the flow of blood from his cut lips. Scowling, he turned upon the speaker.

"Ah, where was yehs when I was doin' all deh fightin'?" he demanded. "Youse kids makes me tired."

"Ah, go ahn!" replied the other argumentatively.

Jimmie replied with heavy contempt. "Ah, youse can't fight, Blue Billie! I kin lick yeh wid one han'."

"Ah, go ahn!" replied Billie again.

"Ah!" said Jimmie threateningly.

"Ah!" said the other in the same tone.

They struck at each other, clinched, and rolled over on the cobble-stones.

"Smash 'im, Jimmie, kick d' face off 'im!" yelled Pete, the lad with the chronic sneer, in tones of delight. The small combatants pounded and kicked, scratched and tore. They began to weep, and their curses struggled in their throats with sobs. The other little boys clasped their hands and wriggled their legs in excitement. They formed a bobbing circle about the pair.

A tiny spectator was suddenly agitated. "Cheese it, Jimmie, cheese it! Here comes yer fader," he yelled. The circle of little boys instantly parted. They drew away and waited in ecstatic awe for that which was about to happen. The two little boys, fighting in the modes of four thousand years ago, did not hear the warning.

Up the avenue there plodded slowly a man with sullen eyes. He was carrying a dinner-pail and smoking an apple-wood pipe. As he neared the spot where the little boys strove, he regarded them listlessly. But suddenly he roared an oath and advanced upon the rolling fighters. "Here, you Jim, git up, now, while I belt yer life out, yeh disorderly brat." He began to kick into the chaotic mass on the ground. The boy Billie felt a heavy boot strike his head. He made a furious effort and disentangled himself from Jimmie. He tottered away.

Jimmie arose painfully from the ground and, confronting his father, began to curse him. His parent kicked him. "Come home, now," he cried, "an' stop yer jawin', er I'll lam the everlasting head off yehs."

They departed. The man paced placidly along with the apple-wood emblem of serenity between his teeth. The boy followed a dozen feet in the rear. He swore luridly, for he felt that it was degradation for one who aimed to be some vague kind of soldier, or a man of blood with a sort of sublime license, to be taken home by a father.*

*Stephen Crane, *op. cit.*, pp. 11-14

1. This selection would lead you to believe that Jimmy was
- a. poor but brave.
- b. not poor but brave.
- c. older and wiser than the rest of the boys.
- d. none of the above.

2. From the story you would feel that Jimmy's father was
- a. a businessman.
- b. dead.
- c. a railroad worker.
- d. none of the above.

3. This story took place in a
- a. rich neighborhood.
- b. poor neighborhood.
- c. suburb.
- d. small town.

4. From what you have read you would believe that Jimmy
- a. loved his father.
- b. had no respect for his father.
- c. didn't see his father too often.
- d. none of the above.

5. The age of the boys in the story was about
- a. 6 to 10 years of age.
- b. 10 to 16.
- c. 17 to 21.
- d. older than the above.

6. The fight took place in
- a. a city park.
- b. an area near the river.
- c. near the railroad tracks.
- d. someone's back yard.

7. The fight between the two rival gangs ended because
- a. Jimmy defeated them all.
- b. The police stopped the fight.
- c. Jimmy's father stopped the fight.
- d. none of the above.

8. Jimmy's education was probably
    a. better than that of the rest of the boys.
    b. no better, but the same, as that of the boys.
    c. less than that of the rest of the boys.
    d. superior to that of the rest of the boys.
9. Jimmy's father, when he met the boys, was probably
    a. on his way to work.
    b. just out for a stroll.
    c. on his way home from work.
    d. driving around in his car.
10. The fight took place
    a. after school.
    b. on a Saturday.
    c. during summer vacation.
    d. at a time not specified in the story.

(*Answers on p. 172*)

Vocabulary Study #2

Following is a list of the more unusual words from the selection you have just read. You will need your dictionary to complete this exercise.

gamins—Fr. *gamin* (street urchin).

precipitately—in a headlong, impetuous manner. L. *praeceps* (headlong).
    What do scientists mean when they try to precipitate precipitation?

ominous—having the character of an evil omen; sinister; menacing; threatening. L. *ominosus* (like an omen).
    What is the difference between:
    ominous   portentous   fateful   foreboding

chronic—lasting for a long time; recurring; perpetual; habitual; constant. Gr. *chronos* (time).

What is the meaning of each of the following
words? Be sure and check them in your dictionary.
chronicle   chronologic   chronological
chronology   chronometer

vainglorious—boastfully vain and proud of oneself; show-
ing or characterized by boastful vanity. L. *vanus*
(empty) and *gloriosus* (full of glory).

contingent—(Adj.) happening by chance; conditional.
(Noun) a proportion or quota; as, a *contingent* of
troops or ships. L. *con* (together) and *tangere* (to
touch).
    Why was the tango so named?
    What is a tangent?
    What do mathematicians mean by a "contingent
    universe"?

catapultian—like a catapult, i.e., a device for shooting or
launching stones, spears, etc. Gr. *kata* (down or
against) and *pallein* (to throw).
    What is the meaning of each of the following
    words? Be sure and check them in your dictionary.
    catachresis   cataclysm   catacomb
    catafalque   catalepsy   catalogue
    catalyst   cataract   catarrh
    catastrophe   catatonic

lurid—vivid in a harsh or shocking way; sensational;
characterized by violent passion or crime, as *lurid*
headlines. L. *luridus* (lurid).

licence (usually spelled *license*)—1. formal authorization.
2. excessive, undisciplined freedom constituting an
abuse of liberty. L. *licere* (to be permitted).
    What is a licentious person?

How to Read a Book Review

Since you are interested enough in reading to purchase this particular book, you are probably interested enough to start building up your own library, if you have not already begun to do so. But a library can be an expensive proposition. The average hardbound book costs about five dollars. Even a meager library of only twenty books represents at least a hundred-dollar investment on your part, so unless you can afford to take chances and buy books sight unseen, you had better cultivate the habit of reading good book reviewers regularly. Despite the rather low esteem in which many authors seem to hold book critics as a class, the average reviewer is a competent professional, usually a writer himself, whose experience and insight can be an invaluable aid in guiding your purchases. (T. S. Eliot claims that the role of the critic is one of the noblest of all—that of protecting the cultural heritage of posterity.)

For a start, read *The New York Times Book Review* and the *Saturday Review*, which offer weekly reviews of a fairly large selection of recently published books. Also, almost any good magazine has a book review section. (Never rely on publishers' announcements or jacket blurbs; they are nothing but sales pitches.)

A standard format for book reviews has evolved which most critics (except such established veterans as Alfred Kazin, Dorothy Parker and Granville Hicks) will invariably adhere to. The first paragraph is a clever introduction. Most reviewers feel obligated to begin by *not* mentioning the book in question, but by discussing some unrelated subject which they use as a lead-in to the actual review. Of course, if you are in a hurry, this part may be skipped. Then follows a summary of the book, and, finally, in the last paragraph, the author's critical opinion. If you already know the general subject of the book, the last paragraph alone will be sufficient for your purposes. (Theater and movie reviews follow quite a different format; the critical opinion is always contained in the very first paragraph, then follows the plot summary, and finally individual criticisms of the actors, director, and so forth.)

Never be satisfied with just one reviewer's opinion, unless you've learned that his tastes always coincide exactly with yours. Just like all other writers, the critic will slant his review according to his own tastes and opinions and those of the publication he is writing for. A book by an ultraconservative politician will probably get quite a different reception in the columns of an ultraconservative magazine, for example, than it will in the pages of an extremely liberal one. Read as many reviews as you can, then, but let them be your guide and not your god. It is your own money that you are spending, and, in the final analysis, it is your own taste that you should follow.

Day VII

Phrase Reading Exercise #5

Western America is one of the most interesting subjects of study the modern world
has seen. There has been nothing in the
past resembling its growth, and probably
there will be nothing in the future. A
vast territory, wonderfully rich in natural re-
sources of many kinds; a temperate and
healthy climate fit for European labour; a
soil generally, and in many places, marvellously,
fertile; in some regions mountains
full of minerals, in others trackless forests
where every tree is over two hundred feet high;
and the whole of this virtually un-
occupied territory thrown open to an energetic race, with all the appliances and
contrivances of modern science at its command, —these are phenomena absolutely
without precedent in history, and which
cannot recur elsewhere, because our planet
contains no such other favoured tract of
country.*

Key-Word Reading Exercise #4

Vague tradition reports that Randolph spoke for three
hours and held his audience; he rarely failed with a Virginian assembly, and in this case his whole career de-
pended on success. Tradition further says that Patrick
Henry remarked to a by-stander, "I haven't seen the

*James Bryce, op. cit., p. 226

little dog before, since he was at school; he was a great atheist then;" and after the speech, shaking hands with his opponent, he added, "Young man, you call me father; then, my son, I have something to say unto thee: *Keep justice, keep truth,*—and you will live to think differently."*

This is what you should have circled:

           tradition   Randolph spoke   three hours   held   audience;   rarely failed   Virginian assembly,   whole career depended   success. Tradition   Patrick Henry remarked   "I haven't seen   since   at school;   great atheist then;"   after   speech,   added,

                                        Keep justice, keep truth,   will live to think differently."

Skipping and Skimming Exercise #4

Question: Who was Freia?
The Rhinegold is the first opera in Richard Wagner's great operatic tetralogy, *The Ring of the Nibelungs.*

The opera is mythical in its setting, and may be briefly summarized as follows: The story opens on the Rhine River, where the three Rhinemaidens are guarding a store of magic gold. The gold would confer all the world's power on its possessor, but to possess it, one must renounce love. Alberich, a dwarf (nibelung) makes advances to the Rhinemaidens and is repulsed. Accordingly, he renounces love and steals the gold.

The scene switches to a mountaintop where Wotan, leader of the gods, dwells. He is contemplating the castle, Valhalla, built for him by giants. The giants, however, have

*Henry Adams, *op. cit.*, p. 36

demanded Freia, a goddess who holds the secret of eternal youth for the gods, as payment for their labors. The giants demand payment, but Wotan and Loge, the god of fire, prevail upon them to accept the Rhinegold instead, if they can produce it by that evening. Loge tricks Alberich and steals the gold from him. Alberich places a curse upon the gold. As soon as the giants are paid, they fight over shares and kill each other, fulfilling the curse. The gods call forth a thunderstorm to clear the air of the murder, then cross over to Valhalla on a rainbow bridge. As they cross the bridge, the Rhinemaidens can be heard in the valley below, castigating the gods for their duplicity, and prophesying the evil that will befall the gods until they restore the gold to its rightful owners.

Critical Reading Exercise #2

In each of the following selections, find the fallacy in reasoning.

1. Your argument holds no water. Everybody knows that Shakespeare was the greatest writer that ever lived, so there's no point in trying to claim that Milton was better.

2. John Doe, star pitcher for last year's American League pennant winners, says that Sta-Smooth hair tonic grooms better and keeps hair neat longer than any other hair tonic on the market.

(*Answers on p. 172*)

Visualizing and Direction-Following Exercise #2

Deal thirteen cards face down in one pile; turn the pile face up and place it at the left to form the stock, deal the fourteenth card face up; this is the first foundation. Place it above and to the right of the stock. Deal four cards face up in a row to the right of the stock, forming the tableau.*

Draw and label the positions of the card:

A—

Your judgment of when to buy, when to _____, and when to _____ should never be dictated by _____ circumstances. Investment should be undertaken only with funds you can honestly and legitimately earmark as _____. With a _____ income and your monthly bills _____, you know where you stand and what amount can be put aside, in reserve, for any _____ opportunity that arises. Or, of course, for _____. A sudden demand for _____ cash should come, if possible, from your _____, not from cashing in your _____.*

(*Answers on p. 172*)

B—

One point should be made _____ at the outset: you don't have to be _____ to invest. Among outsiders you hear it said that stock ownership is a _____ man's game. This can mean any of several things: that the _____ is too complicated for the little man, that brokers aren't interested in _____ orders, that only the person who can lose a bundle without _____ it should invest. However _____ these arguments, they are all _____.*

(*Answers on p. 172*)

*Adolph Suehsdorf, *op. cit.*, pp. 20-21

How to Read Business Material and Textbooks

The type of reading we will discuss today is your bread-and-butter reading—business material and textbooks. Studying or keeping up with the newest developments in your field is usually not a matter of personal choice but a question of necessity. Your advancements, your marks in college, your income, will all depend to a great degree on how well you can read. The man who reads more and reads effectively, who is abreast of the latest innovations in management, production, and products, who can thoroughly grasp the material in a textbook and do collateral reading besides, who isn't at a loss for ideas when he talks with his superiors, is the man who is going to get the promotions, the grades, the money, and ultimately the success. Don't construe this as a general statement that the more you read, the better off you will be. Let us say that the more you read of *what is important to you*, the better off you will be. Obviously, if you are reading for a purpose, whether it is to get ahead in business or in school, you will have to *select* what you read so you won't be wasting your time on nonessentials. No one can disparage the pursuit of knowledge for its own sake, but if your field is marketing and you are interested in advancement, you had better spend more time on the marketing journals than on some other enjoyable but totally irrelevant field.

Selection, then, is the key. And to increase your ability to select, *pre-read*. Here is where the authors of business and college publications work for you. They *write* their material to be pre-read. Almost all publications from the

Harvard Business Review right down to a first-year text in economics make liberal use of visual aids such as bold print, italic print, graphs, charts, etc. They make your job twice as easy. Keeping this in mind, let's go through your approach to this material step by step.

When you first select a book or journal, don't immediately start reading the first page. Try to get an idea of what to expect. Run down the table of contents, to determine the main interests of the publication. Do you know any of the authors? Have you read their material before? What were their views? What would you expect them to say in these articles? Then pick out the sections that are of most interest to you. (Trade journals usually comprise a collection of articles on various topics; textbooks, of course, are usually confined to one major subject.) If you see an article on the dangers of a balance of payments deficit, for instance, and you are quite well versed in the dangers thereof, *don't waste your time on it.* You are not reading to pat yourself on the back because the authors agree with you; you are reading to find authors who *disagree* with you, who can teach you something. When you have picked your spots, as it were, then start to pre-read. Read the bold print first, then the graphs and charts. The old saw says that a picture is worth a thousand words; graphs must be worth much more. For instance, if you are going to read a government pamphlet on the distribution of the economy, look for the graph first. Then *study* it. When you understand the graph, read the last few paragraphs of the article to see if the author draws any conclusions. If he does and you understand them, then you've finished the job and can go on to something else.

If you decide that further reading is warranted, stop and think first. Since the article is in your field, you probably have a grasp of the basic facts before you even start. In that case, use your knowledge; try to *anticipate*. Then read it again all the way through and *fast*. Don't get bogged down in details yet. Understand the article in general terms first. Then see if it is worth your while to learn the details. If it is, then go back and spend the time necessary to memorize them. But one caution here: don't spend time studying what you honestly can't expect to remember. Going back to our pamphlet on the distribution of the economy: even if you feel you should take the time to study it thoroughly, you probably would be wasting your time if you tried to memorize the exact incomes of all the groups represented. Instead, learn, for example, in round figures where farmers' incomes stand in relation to accountants'. That you will probably remember. But the more details you try to commit to memory, the longer it will take you and the greater is the likelihood that you will only succeed in confusing the facts that you could have remembered.

But most important of all, do not read just to be a fact-collector. In school or in business, *all* facts are irrelevant unless you can fit them into a larger context. Compare everything you read, integrate it, organize it. Arrange your facts along the various angles of a question; make them take sides so you can draw conclusions from what you read, so you can develop your own opinions and finally merge all the facts into a clear-cut pattern of action.

Day VIII

Phrase-Reading Exercise #6

The weakness   of Congress   is the strength
    of the President.   Though it cannot be said
    that his office   has risen   in power of
dignity   since 1789,   there are reasons
for believing   that it may reach   a higher
point   than it has occupied   at any time
    since the Civil War.   The tendency everywhere
    in America   to concentrate power
and responsibility   in one man   is unmistak-
able.   There is no danger   that the President
    should become a despot,   that is, should
attempt   to make his will prevail   against the
will   of the majority.   But he may have
    a great part to play   as the leader   of the
majority   and the exponent of its will.   He is
in some respects   better fitted   both to represent   and to influence   public opinion
than Congress is.   No doubt he suffers   from
being the nominee   of a party,   because this
draws   on every act he does   the hostility
    of zealots   of the opposite party.   But the
number   of voters   who are not   party
zealots   increases.*

Skipping and Skimming Exercise #5

*Question: Where may an influenza virus be grown experi-
mentally?*
Much of the recent progress in virology stems from the

*James Bryce, *op. cit.*, pp. 241-2
114

interest generated in viruses by the recent onslaughts of polio and influenza in England and America. One of the major problems confronting the virologist as opposed to the bacteriologist, however, is the semiparasitic nature of the virus. Bacteria can be grown experimentally in tubes of broth or plates of nutrients. Whole colonies can easily be made to thrive in laboratories. The virus, on the other hand, besides being much smaller than most bacteria, is capable of multiplication only within the cells of a living host. Thus, the virologist has to inject mice or chicken embryos or some other obtainable, susceptible host with the virus, and study it by the symptoms it causes in the living creature.

The smallness of the virus is no longer an extreme problem. The electron microscope is capable of producing very detailed pictures of the organism.

Eye-Swing Exercise #5

Critical Reading Exercise #3

In each of the following selections, find the fallacy in reasoning.

1. It is a well-known fact that one of the basic tenets of Fascism is a belief in the supremacy of the state. We have just heard Franz admit that he believes the state should be supreme, not the individual citizen. Obviously, the man is a Fascist.

2. The present situation leaves us with only two alternatives. Either we return to laissez-faire capitalism or we will eventually fall completely under the domination of Communism. The world can now be conceived in terms of black and white—the grays are rapidly disappearing. There is no middle road left, for every time the gray of compromise is swallowed up, it is always by the blacks, the side of the Communists.

(*Answers on p. 172*)

Timed Reading Exercise #3

Pre-read and read the following selection, timing yourself as you read. When you finish, divide the number of minutes it took you into 4,800 words to obtain your words per minute score. By this time, you should strive to keep your time within a maximum limit of twelve minutes. Then answer the questions.

IV

The charm of a single summer day on these island shores is something impossible to express, never to be forgotten. Rarely, in the paler zones, do earth and heaven take such luminosity: those will best understand me who have seen the splendor of a West Indian sky. And yet there is a tenderness of tint, a caress of color, in these Gulf-days which is not of the Antilles,—a spirituality, as of eternal tropical spring. It must have been to even such a sky that Xenophanes lifted up his eyes of old when he vowed the Infinite Blue was God;—it was indeed under such a sky that De Soto named the vastest and grandest of Southern havens Espiritu Santo,—the Bay of the Holy Ghost. There is a something unutterable in this bright Gulf-air that compels awe,—something vital, something holy, something pantheistic: and reverentially the mind asks itself if what the eye beholds is not the Πνευμα indeed, the Infinite Breath, the Divine Ghost, the great Blue Soul of the Unknown. All, all is blue in the calm, —save the low land under your feet, which you almost forget, since it seems only as a tiny green flake afloat in the liquid eternity of day. Then slowly, caressingly, irresistibly, the witchery of the Infinite grows upon you: out of Time and Space you begin to dream with open eyes,— to drift into delicious oblivion of facts,—to forget the past, the present, the substantial,—to comprehend nothing but the existence of that infinite Blue Ghost as something into which you would wish to melt utterly away forever. . . .

And this day-magic of azures endures sometimes for months together. Cloudlessly the dawn reddens up through a violet east: there is no speck upon the blossoming of its Mystical Rose,—unless it be the silhouette of some passing gull, whirling his sickle-wings against the crimsoning. Ever, as the sun floats higher, the flood shifts its color. Sometimes smooth and gray, yet flickering with the morning gold, it is the vision of John,—the apocalyptic Sea of Glass mixed with fire;—again, with the growing breeze, it takes that incredible purple tint familiar mostly to painters of West Indian scenery;—once more, under the blaze of noon, it changes to a waste of broken emerald. With evening, the horizon assumes tints of inexpressible sweetness,—pearl-lights, opaline colors of milk and fire;

117

and in the west are topaz-glowings and wondrous flushings as of nacre. Then, if the sea sleeps, it dreams of all these, —faintly, weirdly,—shadowing them even to the verge of heaven.

Beautiful, too, are those white phantasmagoria which, at the approach of equinoctial days, mark the coming of the winds. Over the rim of the sea a bright cloud gently pushes up its head. It rises; and others rise with it, to right and left—slowly at first; then more swiftly. All are brilliantly white and flocculent, like loose new cotton. Gradually they mount in enormous line high above the Gulf, rolling and wreathing into an arch that expands and advances,—bending from horizon to horizon. A clear, cold breath accompanies its coming. Reaching the zenith, it seems there to hang poised awhile,—a ghostly bridge arching the empyrean,—upreaching its measureless span from either underside of the world. Then the colossal phantom begins to turn, as on a pivot of air,—always preserving its curvilinear symmetry, but moving its unseen ends beyond and below the sky-circle. And at last it floats away unbroken beyond the blue sweep of the world, with a wind following after. Day after day, almost at the same hour, the white arc rises, wheels, and passes. . . .

. . . Never a glimpse of rock on these low shores;— only long sloping beaches and bars of smooth tawny sand. Sand and sea teem with vitality;—over all the dunes there is a constant susurration, a blattering and swarming of crustacea;—through all the sea there is a ceaseless play of silver lightning,—flashing of myriad fish. Sometimes the shallows are thickened with minute, transparent, crablike organisms,—all colorless as gelatine. There are days also when countless medusæ drift in—beautiful veined creatures that throb like hearts, with perpetual systole and diastole of their diaphanous envelops: some, of translucent azure or rose, seem in the flood the shadows or ghosts of huge campanulate flowers;—others have the

118

semblance of strange living vegetables,—great milky tubers, just beginning to sprout. But woe to the human skin grazed by those shadowy sproutings and spectral stamens! —the touch of glowing iron is not more painful. . . . Within an hour or two after their appearance all these tremulous jellies vanish mysteriously as they came.

Perhaps, if a bold swimmer, you may venture out alone a long way—once! Not twice!—even in company. As the water deepens beneath you, and you feel those ascending wave-currents of coldness arising which bespeak profundity, you will also begin to feel innumerable touches, as of groping fingers—touches of the bodies of fish, innumerable fish, fleeing towards shore. The farther you advance, the more thickly you will feel them come; and above you and around you, to right and left, others will leap and fall so swiftly as to daze the sight, like intercrossing fountain-jets of fluid silver. The gulls fly low about you, circling with sinister squeaking cries;—perhaps for an instant your feet touch in the deep something heavy, swift, lithe, that rushes past with a swirling shock. Then the fear of the Abyss, the vast and voiceless Nightmare of the Sea, will come upon you; the silent panic of all those opaline millions that flee glimmering by will enter into you also. . . .

From what do they flee thus perpetually? Is it from the giant sawfish or the ravishing shark?—from the herds of the porpoises, or from the *grande-écaille,*—that splendid monster whom no net may hold,—all helmed and armored in argent plate-mail?—or from the hideous devil-fish of the Gulf,—gigantic, flat-bodied, black, with immense sidefins ever outspread like the pinions of a bat,—the terror of luggermen, the uprooter of anchors? From all these, perhaps, and from other monsters likewise—goblin shapes evolved by Nature as destroyers, as equilibrists, as counterchecks to that prodigious fecundity, which, unhindered, would thicken the deep into one measureless and waveless

ferment of being. . . . But when there are many bathers
these perils are forgotten,—numbers give courage,—one
can abandon one's self, without fear of the invisible, to
the long, quivering, electrical caresses of the sea. . . .

V

Thirty years ago, Last Island lay steeped in the enormous light of even such magical days. July was dying;—
for weeks no fleck of cloud had broken the heaven's blue
dream of eternity; winds held their breath; slow wavelets
caressed the bland brown beach with a sound as of kisses
and whispers. To one who found himself alone, beyond
the limits of the village and beyond the hearing of its
voices,—the vast silence, the vast light, seemed full of
weirdness. And these hushes, these transparencies, do not
always inspire a causeless apprehension: they are omens
sometimes—omens of coming tempest. Nature,—incomprehensible Sphinx!—before her mightiest bursts of rage,
ever puts forth her divinest witchery, makes more manifest
her awful beauty. . . .

But in that forgotten summer the witchery lasted many
long days,—days born in rose-light, buried in gold. It was
the height of the season. The long myrtle-shadowed village
was thronged with its summer population;—the big hotel
could hardly accommodate all its guests;—the bathing-
houses were too few for the crowds who flocked to the
water morning and evening. There were diversions for
all,—hunting and fishing parties, yachting excursions,
rides, music, games, promenades. Carriage wheels flickering along the beach, seaming its smoothness noiselessly, as
if muffled. Love wrote its dreams upon the sand. . . .

. . . Then one great noon, when the blue abyss of day
seemed to yawn over the world more deeply than ever
before, a sudden change touched the quicksilver smoothness of the waters—the swaying shadow of a vast motion.

First the whole sea-circle appeared to rise up bodily at the sky; the horizon-curve lifted to a straight line; the line darkened and approached,—a monstrous wrinkle, an immeasurable fold of green water, moving swift as a cloud-shadow pursued by sunlight. But it had looked formidable only by startling contrast with the previous placidity of the open: it was scarcely two feet high;—it curled slowly as it neared the beach, and combed itself out in sheets of woolly foam with a low, rich roll of whispered thunder. Swift in pursuit another followed—a third —a feebler fourth; then the sea only swayed a little, and stilled again. Minutes passed, and the immeasurable heaving recommenced—one, two, three, four . . . seven long swells this time;—and the Gulf smoothed itself once more. Irregularly the phenomenon continued to repeat itself, each time with heavier billowing and briefer intervals of quiet—until at last the whole sea grew restless and shifted color and flickered green;—the swells became shorter and changed form. Then from horizon to shore ran one uninterrupted heaving—one vast green swarming of snaky shapes, rolling in to hiss and flatten upon the sand. Yet no single cirrus-speck revealed itself through all the violet heights: there was no wind!—you might have fancied the sea had been upheaved from beneath. . . .

And indeed the fancy of a seismic origin for a windless surge would not appear in these latitudes to be utterly without foundation. On the fairest days a southeast breeze may bear you an odor singular enough to startle you from sleep,—a strong, sharp smell as of fish-oil; and gazing at the sea you might be still more startled at the sudden apparition of great oleaginous patches spreading over the water, sheeting over the swells. That is, if you had never heard of the mysterious submarine oil-wells, the volcanic fountains, unexplored, that well up with the eternal pulsing of the Gulf-Stream. . . .

But the pleasure-seekers of Last Island knew there

must have been a "great blow" somewhere that day. Still the sea swelled; and a splendid surf made the evening bath delightful. Then, just at sundown, a beautiful cloud-bridge grew up and arched the sky with a single span of cottony pink vapor, that changed and deepened color with the dying of the iridescent day. And the cloud-bridge approached, stretched, strained, and swung round at last to make way for the coming of the gale,—even as the light bridges that traverse the dreamy Têche swing open when luggermen sound through their conch-shells the long, bellowing signal of approach.

Then the wind began to blow, with the passing of July. It blew from the northeast, clear, cool. It blew in enormous sighs, dying away at regular intervals, as if pausing to draw breath. All night it blew; and in each pause could be heard the answering moan of the rising surf,—as if the rhythm of the sea moulded itself after the rhythm of the air,—as if the waving of the water responded precisely to the waving of the wind,—a billow for every puff, a surge for every sigh.

The August morning broke in a bright sky;—the breeze still came cool and clear from the northeast. The waves were running now at a sharp angle to the shore: they began to carry fleeces, an innumerable flock of vague green shapes, wind-driven to be despoiled of their ghostly wool. Far as the eye could follow the line of the beach, all the slope was white with the great shearing of them. Clouds came, flew as in a panic against the face of the sun, and passed. All that day and through the night and into the morning again the breeze continued from the northeast, blowing like an equinoctial gale. . . .

Then day by day the vast breath freshened steadily, and the waters heightened. A week later sea-bathing had become perilous: colossal breakers were herding in, like moving leviathan-backs, twice the height of a man. Still the gale grew, and the billowing waxed mightier, and

122

faster and faster overhead flew the tatters of torn cloud. The gray morning of the 9th wanly lighted a surf that appalled the best swimmers: the sea was one wild agony of foam, the gale was rending off the heads of the waves and veiling the horizon with a fog of salt spray. Shadowless and gray the day remained; there were mad bursts of lashing rain. Evening brought with it a sinister apparition, looming through a cloud-rent in the west—a scarlet sun in a green sky. His sanguine disk, enormously magnified, seemed barred like the body of a belted planet. A moment, and the crimson spectre vanished; and the moonless night came.

Then the Wind grew weird. It ceased being a breath; it became a Voice moaning across the world,—hooting,—uttering nightmare sounds,—*Whoo!—whoo!—whoo!*—and with each stupendous owl-cry the mooing of the waters seemed to deepen, more and more abysmally, through all the hours of darkness. From the northwest the breakers of the bay began to roll high over the sandy slope, into the salines;—the village bayou broadened to a bellowing flood. . . . So the tumult swelled and the turmoil heightened until morning,—a morning of gray gloom and whistling rain. Rain of bursting clouds and rain of wind-blown brine from the great spuming agony of the sea.

The steamer *Star* was due from St. Mary's that fearful morning. Could she come? No one really believed it,—no one. And nevertheless men struggled to the roaring beach to look for her, because hope is stronger than reason. . . .

Even to-day, in these Creole islands, the advent of the steamer is the great event of the week. There are no telegraph lines, no telephones: the mail-packet is the only trustworthy medium of communication with the outer world, bringing friends, news, letters. The magic of steam has placed New Orleans nearer to New York than to the Timbaliers, nearer to Washington than to Wine Island, nearer to Chicago than to Barataria Bay. And even during the deepest sleep of waves and winds there will come betimes to sojourners in this unfamiliar archipelago a feeling of lonesomeness that is a fear, a feeling of isolation from the world of men,—totally unlike that sense of solitude which haunts one in the silence of mountain-heights, or amid the eternal tumult of lofty granitic coasts: a sense of helpless insecurity. The land seems but an undulation of the sea-bed: its highest ridges do not rise more than the height of a man above the salines on either side;—the salines themselves lie almost level with the level of the floodtides;—the tides are variable, treacherous, mysterious. But when all around and above these ever-changing shores the twin vastnesses of heaven and sea begin to utter the tremendous revelation of themselves as infinite forces in contention, then indeed this sense of separation from humanity appals. . . . Perhaps it was such a feeling which forced men, on the tenth day of August, eighteen hundred and fifty-six, to hope against hope for the coming of the *Star*, and to strain their eyes towards far-off Terrebonne. "It was a wind you could lie down on," said my friend the pilot.

. . . "Great God!" shrieked a voice above the shouting of the storm,—*"she is coming!"* . . . It was true. Down the Atchafalaya, and thence through strange mazes of bayou, lakelet, and pass, by a rear route familiar only to the best of pilots, the frail river-craft had toiled into Caillou Bay, running close to the main shore;—and now she was heading right for the island, with the wind aft, over the monstrous sea. On she came, swaying, rocking, plunging,—with a great whiteness wrapping her about like a cloud, and moving with her moving,—a tempest-whirl of spray;—ghost-white and like a ghost she came, for her smoke-stacks exhaled no visible smoke—the wind devoured it! The excitement on shore became wild;—men shouted themselves hoarse; women laughed and cried.

Every telescope and opera-glass was directed upon the coming apparition; all wondered how the pilot kept his feet; all marvelled at the madness of the captain.

But Captain Abraham Smith was not mad. A veteran American sailor, he had learned to know the great Gulf as scholars know deep books by heart: he knew the birthplace of its tempests, the mystery of its tides, the omens of its hurricanes. While lying at Brashear City he felt the storm had not yet reached its highest, vaguely foresaw a mighty peril, and resolved to wait no longer for a lull. "Boys," he said, "we've got to take her out in spite of Hell!" And they "took her out." Through all the peril, his men stayed by him and obeyed him. By mid-morning the wind had deepened to a roar,—lowering sometimes to a rumble, sometimes bursting upon the ears like a measureless and deafening crash. Then the captain knew the *Star* was running a race with Death. "She'll win it," he muttered;—"She'll stand it.... Perhaps they'll have need of me to-night."

She won! With a sonorous steam-chant of triumph the brave little vessel rode at last into the bayou, and anchored hard by her accustomed resting-place, in full view of the hotel, though not near enough to shore to lower her gang-plank. . . . But she had sung her swan-song. Gathering in from the northeast, the waters of the bay were already marbling over the salines and half across the island; and still the wind increased its paroxysmal power.

Cottages began to rock. Some slid away from the solid props upon which they rested. A chimney tumbled. Shutters were wrenched off; verandas demolished. Light roofs lifted, dropped again, and flapped into ruin. Trees bent their heads to the earth. And still the storm grew louder and blacker with every passing hour.

The *Star* rose with the rising of the waters, dragging her anchor. Two more anchors were put out, and still she dragged—dragged in with the flood,—twisting, shuddering, careening in her agony. Evening fell; the sand began to move with the wind, stinging faces like a continuous fire of fine shot; and frenzied blasts came to buffet the steamer forward, sideward. Then one of her hog-chains parted with a clang like the boom of a big bell. Then another! ... Then the captain bade his men to cut away all her upper works, clean to the deck. Overboard into the seething went her stacks, her pilot-house, her cabins,— and whirled away. And the naked hull of the *Star*, still dragging her three anchors, labored on through the darkness, nearer and nearer to the immense silhouette of the hotel, whose hundred windows were now all aflame. The vast timber building seemed to defy the storm. The wind, roaring round its broad verandas,—hissing through every crevice with the sound and force of steam,—appeared to waste its rage. And in the half-lull between two terrible gusts there came to the captain's ears a sound that seemed strange in that night of multitudinous terrors ... a sound of music!

VI

... Almost every evening throughout the season there had been dancing in the great hall;—there was dancing that night also. The population of the hotel had been augmented by the advent of families from other parts of the island, who found their summer cottages insecure places of shelter: there were nearly four hundred guests assembled. Perhaps it was for this reason that the entertainment had been prepared upon a grander plan than usual, that it assumed the form of a fashionable ball. And all those pleasure-seekers,—representing the wealth and beauty of the Creole parishes,—whether from Ascension or Assumption, St. Mary's or St. Landry's, Iberville or Terrebonne, whether inhabitants of the multi-colored and many-balconied Creole quarter of the quaint metropolis, or dwellers in the dreamy paradises of the Têche,—mingled joyously, knowing each other, feeling in some sort akin—whether affiliated by blood, connaturalized by caste, or simply interassociated by traditional sympathies of class sentiment and class interest. Perhaps in the more than ordinary merriment of that evening something of nervous exaltation might have been discerned,—something like a feverish resolve to oppose apprehension with gayety, to combat uneasines by diversion. But the hours passed in mirthfulness; the first general feeling of depression began to weigh less and less upon the guests; they had found reason to confide in the solidity of the massive building; there were no positive terrors, no outspoken fears; and the new conviction of all had found expression in the words of the host himself,—*"Il n'ya rien de mieux à faire que de s'amuser!"* Of what avail to lament the prospective devastation of cane-fields,—to discuss the possible ruin of crops? Better to seek solace in choreographic harmonies, in the rhythm of gracious motion and of perfect melody, than hearken to the discords of the wild orchestra of storms;—wiser to admire the grace of Parisian toilets, the eddy of trailing robes with its fairy-foam of lace, the ivorine loveliness of glossy shoulders and jewelled throats, the glimmering of satin-slippered feet,—than to watch the raging of the flood without, or the flying of the wrack. . . .

So the music and the mirth went on: they made joy for themselves—those elegant guests;—they jested and sipped riched wines;—they pledged, and hoped, and loved, and promised, with never a thought of the morrow, on the night of the tenth of August, eighteen hundred and fifty-six. Observant parents were there, planning for the future bliss of their nearest and dearest;—mothers and fathers of handsome lads, lithe and elegant as young pines, and fresh from the polish of foreign university training;—mothers and fathers of splendid girls whose simplest attitudes were

127

witcheries. Young cheeks flushed, young hearts fluttered with an emotion more puissant than the excitement of the dance;—young eyes betrayed the happy secret discreeter lips would have preserved. Slave-servants circled through the aristocratic press, bearing dainties and wines, praying permision to pass in terms at once humble and officious,—always in the excellent French which well-trained house-servants were taught to use on such occasions.

... Night wore on: still the shining floor palpitated to the feet of the dancers; still the pianoforte pealed, and still the violins sang,—and the sound of their singing shrilled through the darkness, in gasps of the gale, to the ears of Captain Smith, as he strove to keep his footing on the spray-drenched deck of the *Star*.

—"Christ!" he muttered,—"a dance! If that wind whips round south, there'll be another dance! ... But I guess the *Star* will stay." ...

Half an hour might have passed; still the lights flamed calmly, and the violins trilled, and the perfumed whirl went on. ... And suddenly the wind veered!

Again the *Star* reeled, and shuddered, and turned, and began to drag all her anchors. But she now dragged away from the great building and its lights,—away from the voluptuous thunder of the grand piano,—even at that moment outpouring the great joy of Weber's melody orchestrated by Berlioz: *l'Invitation à la Valse,*—with its marvellous musical swing!

—"Waltzing!" cried the captain. "God help them!—God help us all now! ... *The Wind waltzes to-night, with the Sea for his partner!*" ...

O the stupendous Valse-Tourbillon! O the mighty Dancer! One—two—three! From northeast to east, from east to southeast, from southeast to south: then from the south he came, whirling the Sea in his arms. ...

... Some one shrieked in the midst of the revels;—

some girl who found her pretty slippers wet. What could it be? Thin streams of water were spreading over the level planking,—curling about the feet of the dancers. . . . What could it be? All the land had begun to quake, even as, but a moment before, the polished floor was trembling to the pressure of circling steps;—all the building shook now; every beam uttered its groan. What could it be? . . .

There was a clamor, a panic, a rush to the windy night. Infinite darkness above and beyond; but the lantern-beams danced far out over an unbroken circle of heaving and swirling black water. Stealthily, swiftly, the measureless sea-flood was rising.

—"Messieurs—mesdames, ce n'est rien. Nothing serious, ladies, I assure you. . . . Mais nous en avons vu bien souvent, les inondations comme celle-ci; ça passe vite! The water will go down in a few hours, ladies;—it never rises higher than this; il n'y a pas le moindre danger, je vous dis! Allons! il n'y a— My God! what is that?" . . .

For a moment there was a ghastly hush of voices. And through that hush there burst upon the ears of all a fearful and unfamiliar sound, as of a colossal cannonade—rolling up from the south, with volleying lightnings. Vastly and swiftly, nearer and nearer it came,—a ponderous and unbroken thunder-roll, terrible as the long muttering of an earthquake.

The nearest mainland,—across mad Caillou Bay to the sea-marshes,—lay twelve miles north; west, by the Gulf, the nearest solid ground was twenty miles distant. There were boats, yes!—but the stoutest swimmer might never reach them now! . . .

Then rose a frightful cry,—the hoarse, hideous, indescribable cry of hopeless fear,—the despairing animal-cry man utters when suddenly brought face to face with Nothingness, without preparation, without consolation, without possibility of respite. . . . Sauve qui peut! Some wrenched

129

down the doors; some clung to the heavy banquet-tables, to the sofas, to the billiard tables:—during one terrible instant,—against fruitless heroisms, against futile generosities,—raged all the frenzy of selfishness, all the brutalities of panic. And then—then came, thundering through the blackness, the giant swells, boom on boom! ... One crash! —the huge frame building rocks like a cradle, seesaws, crackles. What are human shrieks now?—the tornado is shrieking! Another!—chandeliers splinter; lights are dashed out; a sweeping cataract hurls in; the immense hall rises,—oscillates,—twirls as upon a pivot,—crepitates,—crumbles into ruin. Crash again!—the swirling wreck dissolves into the wallowing of another monster billow; and a hundred cottages overturn, spin in sudden eddies, quiver, disjoint, and melt into the seething.

... So the hurricane passed,—tearing off the heads of the prodigious waves, to hurl them a hundred feet in air, —heaping up the ocean against the land,—upturning the woods. Bays and passes were swollen to abysses; rivers regorged; the sea-marshes were changed to raging wastes of water. Before New Orleans the flood of the mile-broad Mississippi rose six feet above highest water-mark. One hundred and ten miles away, Donaldsonville trembled at the towering tide of the Lafourche. Lakes strove to burst their boundaries. Far-off river steamers tugged wildly at their cables,—shivering like tethered creatures that hear by night the approaching howl of destroyers. Smoke-stacks were hurled overboard, pilot-houses torn away, cabins blown to fragments.

And over roaring Kaimbuck Pass,—over the agony of Caillou Bay,—the billowing tide rushed unresisted from the Gulf,—tearing and swallowing the land in its course, —ploughing out deep-sea channels where sleek herds had been grazing but a few hours before,—rending islands in twain,—and ever bearing with it, through the night, enormous vortex of wreck and vast wan drift of corpses. ...

But the *Star* remained. And Captain Abraham Smith, with a long, good rope about his waist, dashed again and again into that awful surging to snatch victims from death, —clutching at passing hands, heads, garments, in the cataract-sweep of the seas,—saving, aiding, cheering, though blinded by spray and battered by drifting wreck, until his strength failed in the unequal struggle at last, and his men drew him aboard senseless, with some beautiful half-drowned girl safe in his arms. But well-nigh twoscore souls had been rescued by him; and the *Star* stayed on through it all.

Long years after, the weed-grown ribs of her graceful skeleton could still be seen, curving up from the sand-dunes of Last Island, in valiant witness of how well she stayed.

VII

Day breaks through the flying wrack, over the infinite heaving of the sea, over the low land made vast with desolation. It is a spectral dawn: a wan light, like the light of a dying sun.

The wind has waned and veered; the flood sinks slowly back to its abysses—abandoning its plunder,—scattering its piteous waifs over bar and dune, over shoal and marsh, among the silences of the mango-swamps, over the long low reaches of sand-grasses and drowned weeds, for more than a hundred miles. From the shell-reefs of Pointe-au-Fer to the shallows of Pelto Bay the dead lie mingled with the high-heaped drift;—from their cypress groves the vultures rise to dispute a share of the feast with the shrieking frigate-birds and squeaking gulls. And as the tremendous tide withdraws its plunging waters, all the pirates of air follow the great white-gleaming retreat: a storm of billowing wings and screaming throats.

And swift in the wake of gull and frigate-bird the Wreckers come, the Spoilers of the dead,—savage skimmers of the sea,—hurricane-riders wont to spread their canvas-pinions in the face of storms; Sicilian and Corsican outlaws, Manila-men from the marshes, deserters from many navies, Lascars, marooners, refugees of a hundred nationalities,—fishers and shrimpers by name, smugglers by opportunity,—wild channel-finders from obscure bayous and unfamiliar *chénières*, all skilled in the mysteries of these mysterious waters beyond the comprehension of the oldest licensed pilot. . . .

There is plunder for all—birds and men. There are drowned sheep in multitude, heaped carcasses of kine. There are casks of claret and kegs of brandy and legions of bottles bobbing in the surf. There are billiard-tables overturned upon the sand;—there are sofas, pianos, footstools and music-stools, luxurious chairs, lounges of bamboo. There are chests of cedar, and toilet-tables of rosewood, and trunks of fine stamped leather stored with precious apparel. There are *objets de luxe* innumerable. There are children's playthings: French dolls in marvellous toilets, and toy carts, and wooden horses, and wooden spades, and brave little wooden ships that rode out the gale in which the great *Nautilus* went down. There is money in notes and in coin—in purses, in pocketbooks, and in pockets: plenty of it! There are silks, satins, laces, and fine linen to be stripped from the bodies of the drowned,—and necklaces, bracelets, watches, finger-rings and fine chains, brooches and trinkets. . . . *"Chi bidizza! —Oh! chi bedda mughieri! Eccu! la bidizza!"* That ball-dress was made in Paris by— But you never heard of him, Sicilian Vicenzu. . . . *"Che bella sposina!"* Her betrothal ring will not come off, Giuseppe; but the delicate bones snap easily: your oyster-knife can sever the tendon. . . . *"Guardate! chi bedda picciota!"* Over her heart you will find it, Valentino—the locket held by that fine Swiss chain of woven hair—*"Caya manan!"* And it is not your quadroon bondsmaid, sweet lady, who now disrobes you so roughly; those Malay hands are less deft than hers,— but she slumbers very far away from you, and may not be aroused from her sleep. *"Na quita mo! dalaga!—na quita maganda!"* . . . Juan, the fastenings of those diamond ear-drops are much too complicated for your peon fingers: tear them out!—*"Dispense, chulita!"* . . .

. . . Suddenly a long, mighty silver trilling fills the ears of all: there is a wild hurrying and scurrying; swiftly, one after another, the overburdened luggers spread wings and flutter away.

Thrice the great cry rings rippling through the gray air, and over the green sea, and over the far-flooded shell-reefs, where the huge white flashes are,—sheet-lightning of breakers,—and over the weird wash of corpses coming in.

It is the steam-call of the relief-boat, hastening to rescue the living, to gather in the dead.

The tremendous tragedy is over!*

1. When did the story take place?
   a. winter.
   b. summer.
   c. spring.
   d. not indicated.

2. The author feels that the place he is describing is probably a bit like
   a. the South Pacific.
   b. Africa.
   c. the West Indies.
   d. none of the above.

*Lafcadio Hearn, *op. cit.*, pp. 29-52

3. In describing the beach area, the author remarks that
   it is
   a. very lonely.
   b. crowded with young people.
   c. very rocky.
   d. swarming with crustacea.

4. The author states that a swimmer should
   a. not venture into these waters.
   b. go in, but only once.
   c. swim regularly in these waters.
   d. none of the above.

5. The author states that the days in this area are
   a. warm with a sky that is blue for months at a time.
   b. interrupted by violent storms.
   c. always hot.
   d. monotonous because they are so clear.

6. The sky, according to the author, seems to
   a. stay blue all day.
   b. shift its color according to the time of day.
   c. stay blue then turn red at dusk.
   d. change color violently.

7. The land, as one looks out on the sea, seems
   a. like a tiny green flake compared to the sea.
   b. to challenge the sea to engulf it.
   c. inconsequential.
   d. none of the above.

8. This selection describes
   a. the land, sea and sky.
   b. just the sky.
   c. mostly the sea, but all three.
   d. mostly the land.

9. There is little or no mention of
   a. birds.
   b. fish.
   c. people.
   d. boats.

10. From this selection you would conclude that the author
    a. is quite taken by this place.
    b. would like to visit it, but hate to live there.
    c. dislikes the place.
    d. wants it all for himself.

(*Answers on p. 172*)

Vocabulary Study #3

Following is a list of the more unusual words from the selection you have just read. You will need your dictionary to complete this exercise.

luminosity—quality of being luminous, giving off light. L. *lumen* (light).

> What is the meaning of each of the following words? Be sure and check them in your dictionary.

lumen	luminary	luminesce
luminescence	luminiferous	

pantheistic—pertaining to the belief that God is the universe and everything in the universe is part of God. Gr. *pan* (all) and *theos* (God).

> What is the meaning of each of the following words? Be sure and check them in your dictionary.

atheism	monotheism	Pan-American
polytheism	theology	theosophy

oblivion—condition of being forgotten. L. *oblivisci* (to forget).

What is an oblivious person?

azure—sky blue.

apocalyptic—of, like, or conveying a revelation. The Apocalypse was the last prophetic book of the New Testament.

opaline—(Adj.) like an opal. (Noun) translucent, milky variety of glass.

nacre—a small shellfish yielding mother-of-pearl.

phantasmagoria—a rapid changing cycle of things seen or imagined, as the figures or events of a dream. Gr. *phantasma* (phantasm) and *agora* (assembly).

What is the meaning of each of the following words? Be sure and check them in your dictionary.
phantasm   phantasmal   phantasy
What is the origin of the word "fantastic"?

equinoctial—pertaining to the time of the equinox, when night and day are equal in length. L. *aequus* (equal) and *nox* (night).

Define the following words. Be sure and check them in your dictionary.
equable   equalitarian   equanimity
equate   equilibrate   equitable
equivocal   equivocate   nocturn
nocturnal   nocturne

flocculent—fluffy; woolly. L. *floccus* (flock of wool).

empyrean—the highest heaven. Gr. *empyrios, en* (in) and *pyr* (fire).
> Could a pyromaniac ever have pyrophobia? What is Pyrex?

susurration—whispering. L. *susurrus* (a whisper).

Crustacea—a class of hard-shelled Arthropoda, including shrimps, crabs, lobsters, etc.

systole—the usual rhythmic contraction of the heart; opposite of the diastole, which is the expansion of the heart. Gr. *syn* (together) and *stellein* (to place).
> Find the meanings and roots of the following words. Be sure and check them in your dictionary.

symbiosis	synapse	synod
symbolism	synchronize	synonym
symmetrical	syncopate	syntax
symphony	syndicate	synthesis
sympodium	syndrome	

diaphanous—transparent or translucent, as gauzy cloth. Gr. *dia* (through) and *phainein* (to show).
> What is a dialectic? What did Marx mean by "dialectical materialism"?

spectral—ghostlike. L. *spectrum* (image), *specere* (to look).
> Is it worthwhile to speculate on the existence of specters?

stamens—pollen-bearing organs of flowers.

tremulous—trembling; quivering; fearful. L. *tremere* (to tremble).
> What is tremendous about an earthquake?
> What is a tremolo?

profundity—state of great depth; physical depth; depth of meaning, as a *profound* statement. L. *profundus* (deep).

argent—(Obs.) silver.

equilibrists—see *equinoctial* above.

prodigious—wonderful; marvelous; enormous. L. *prodigiosus* (marvelous).
> Would it be sad if a prodigy were prodigal with his talents?
> Both *prodigy* and *prodigal* have different roots. What do they mean?

fecundity—the quality or power of being fecund; fruitfulness; productiveness. L. *fecundus* (fertile).
> How does a nation's fertility rate differ from its fecundity rate?

How to Read Business Letters

The business letter is one of the most maligned institutions of our day. True, it does seem reasonable that all the "pursuant to" and "in reference to yours of" phrases could be dropped in favor of plain English, but it must be remembered that the business letter of today serves several other purposes besides simple communication. First of all, it creates *uniformity,* and uniformity, some say, is far more in the interest of a large corporation than excessive individuality. And second, it gives *anonymity.* A skillfully written business letter with its preponderance of impersonal constructions ("It is felt that . . . " rather than "*I* feel that . . . ") makes it difficult to place blame and easy to claim praise. But, granted the usefulness of the modern business letter, the fact remains that too often it is extremely difficult or boring to read.

Your method of reading business letters will differ according to your particular job situation. If you customarily receive just one or two a day, you may as well take the trouble to read them all the way through. (Most business letters are reasonably short.) But, as is more likely the case, if you have to wade through a whole stack of letters every day, some short cuts are in order.

Riffle through the whole pile of letters, looking at the letterheads. Deposit those from correspondents in whom you are definitely not interested in a file next to your desk. Then, very quickly, glance at the *second* paragraph of those that are left. The first paragraph of a business letter will usually be a friendly hello. In most cases the only item of importance in the first paragraph will be the statement that the letter is written in answer to a letter of yours; this reference is usually made in the very first line. Again, separate those you definitely are not interested in from those that might be important. Read this latter pile thoroughly—by this time it should be a very small pile. Needless to say, if you have any doubt at all about the importance of a letter, don't discard it until you have made sure. But by breaking the habit of automatically reading thoroughly *everything* that comes across your desk, you can save a tremendous amount of time.

One final point. You can also do your part to cut down on the amount of unnecessary business correspondence. Up to 15 per cent of all business letters are written because a previous letter was not properly understood. Make sure your own letters do their job on the first time around. Avoid long (and usually insincere) over-friendly or fawning salutations. State your business, and get to the point immediately. Keep your sentences short, concise and crisp. And, unless you have good reason not to, avoid the language of business—"businessese," one writer called it. Just use plain English, as you do when you speak, and instead of getting a lot of questioning replies in return, you'll get results.

On the next page is a typical business letter. Observe its structure and where the important information is contained.

National Tires Inc.
202 S. Broad St.
Metropolis, N. Y.
February 8, 1964

John W. Arden
Purchasing Manager
Swann's Inc.
333 Erie Ave.
Deertown, Pa.

Dear Mr. Arden:

Thank you for your letter of 1/22. I have checked into the matter personally, and will see that your shipment is expedited.

I am sure that you do understand that your order was delayed because of the recent dock workers' strike. However, you may now expect shipment of the tires you ordered (160 7-15-50 nylon sure-tread) by 2/15 at the latest.

I hope that date meets with your satisfaction. Allow me to apologize again for the delay.

Sincerely,
James H. Foxe
Delivery Manager

JHF/bg

Notice that in the above letter, the important information was contained in the last line of the second paragraph. The man receiving the letter would be interested in the date of shipment, not the reasons for the delay. Once he sees "letter of 1/22" (he then knows why the man is writing, if he didn't from the letterhead), he has only to find "2/15 at the latest," and his job is finished. Since a business letter rarely is concerned with more than one topic, this technique of skimming will be adequate for most of your mail.

Day IX

Eye-Swing Exercise #6

Critical Reading Exercise #4

In the following selection circle the emotionally charged words and phrases. Is there a fallacy in the reasoning, or implied reasoning?

Let's consider the facts. Progressive education succeeded in worming its way into the nation's school systems some thirty years ago. Since that time, with the help of the egghead professors in the teacher factories, it has gained a strangle hold on American youth. I said we'd look at the facts. All right, let's look at the incidence of juvenile delinquency in the major cities. Lately, the kids have taken to roaming in "wolf-packs," bloodthirsty hordes of pimpled sadists, a throwback to cave-man days. Is this where the so-called "progressive" education has taken us? I say it's high time we got back to the good old three R's. Maybe the $20,000-a-year eggheads in their university ivory towers will think that's naive, but kids in my day at least learned respect for their home and family; they learned to love religion and act like decent citizens, *not* how to use a switchblade!

(*Answers on p. 172*)

Paragraph Development Exercise #3

Rearrange the sentences* in the proper order. What is the topic sentence of each group?

A—
1. But it had no intention of allowing the colonists to escape taxation permanently.
2. Repealed them, that is, except for the tax on tea, which a stubborn monarch, George III, insisted on retaining as a mark of Parliamentary authority.

*Paul M. Angle, *op. cit.*, pp. 136, 140

3. In the face of united opposition, the British government retreated.
4. In 1767 it passed the Townshend Acts, levying certain customs duties in addition to those already in force, only to repeal the Acts when the Americans refused to import British goods.
5. In March, 1766, Parliament repealed the Stamp Act.

(Answers on p. 173)

B—
1. Minutemen, pledged to spring to arms at a minute's warning, drilled on the village greens.
2. Warned by Paul Revere and William Dawes, the militia assembled under arms at Lexington, five miles east of Concord.
3. In mid-April, 1775, the British commander in Boston heard a report that arms were being collected at Concord, some twenty miles northwest of the city.
4. Relations between England and the colonies steadily became worse.
5. The British retaliated by closing the Massachusetts ports to shipping and stationing troops there.
6. On the evening of the 18th he dispatched a force of 700 regulars to destroy the stores.
7. Bostonians pitched a cargo of tea into the harbor.

(Answers on p. 173)

Sentence Correction Exercise #4

Find the illogical word in each sentence and replace it with the logical one.
1. The fact that cancer has been induced in mice by subjecting them to applications of cigarette tars does not

necessarily disprove the hypothesis that smoking causes cancer in humans.

2. Mythologies, of course, are just that—pure fable, but because they are so inextricably entwined with the psychology of a particular ethnic group, they are of little value to the anthropologist.

3. Amazingly enough, Spanish explorers in what is now the Los Angeles area reported the incidence of smog. It is then highly possible that automobiles and factories are the chief reason for its occurrence.

4. Old English was replete with inflected forms of common words; that is, suffixes would be added to words to indicate gender, number, case, and so on. Modern English is so streamlined because these forms have been largely retained.

5. When one engages the services of a professional man, he should consider that the fee charged will be in some degree compensation for the many years necessary for the individual to achieve his present professional status. It is entirely improper to base fees on the long time necessary to prepare to provide a service.

(Answers on p. 173)

Vocabulary

As an English-speaking people, we have been endowed with one of the most beautiful, expressive and complete languages in the world. English derives a great deal of its flexibility and expressiveness from the fact that it is actually an amalgam of many languages of the world, particularly of the Romance languages (Italian, French, etc.), the Germanic tongues, and the ancient Greek. To go even further back, we can see that English is a modern-day descendant of the ancient Indo-European dialects which fathered a large group of languages stretching from India to the British Isles. One characteristic of this language family is that it is *inflectional;* that is, the meaning of a word is expressed by combining the word root with significant *affixes* (elements added to the beginning or end of the word). Since the Latin, Germanic, and Greek languages were all very highly inflected, English still bears this stamp, although the imprint is somewhat fading.

Now that you have set yourself seriously to the task of improving your vocabulary, you will greatly facilitate the job by taking into account this structural quality of the language. Rather than simply learning a word, learn how it is *made.* Understand the meaning of its root and the change wrought upon it by its *affix,* either *prefix* (an affix at the beginning of a word) or *suffix* (an affix at the end of a word). Knowledge of word structure and the meaning of the most common roots and affixes will enable you to discern the meaning of many words even though you have never seen them before. The rest of this chapter will be devoted to exercises to improve this ability.

These are some of the most important roots and affixes:

Roots

ag, actus—to do, move, urge
aud, audit—to hear
cap, capt, cip, cept—to take, seize, hold
ced, cess—to go, yield
leg, lect—to read, gather
mitt, miss—to send, throw
pell, puls—to drive
roga—to ask, propose
sent, sens—to feel, perceive
vid, vis—to see

Prefixes

a, ab, abs—away from
a, ad—to
ante—before
ben, bene—well
co, com, con—with
de—down, from, away
di, dif, dis—apart, from, away, not
e, ex—out
in, im—in, into, toward
in—not
ob—against, toward, reversely
per—through
syn, syl, sym—along with, together

Suffixes

age—act or state of
esce, escent, escence—becoming
fic, fy—to make
ism—act of, manner of, state of

The following exercises are designed to develop your understanding of the structure of words and their roots and affixes. Use the root or affix indicated above each exercise to form the words which should be inserted in the blanks. Definitions of the desired words are listed below each exercise.

ROOT—AG, ACTUS

1. It appears as though the United States and Russia may ____(a)____finally agree on a test ban treaty. Representatives of the two countries met to____(b)____the proposals, thereby bringing the world one step closer to making what was for so long a dream an____(c)____.

2. According to the most reliable____(d)____tables, the more____(e)____a person is, the longer he will live.
   (a) really
   (b) set in motion
   (c) reality
   (d) calculations of risk and rate
   (e) having a tendency toward action

(*Answers on p. 173*)

ROOT—AUD, AUDIT

1. The aspirants gathered in the____(a)____for their ____(b)____. Among the____(c)____was a famous producer. Whatever the young singers lacked in proficiency, they made up for with an enthusiasm that sometimes placed a strain on the____(d)____organs of the____(e)____.
   (a) a hall for performances or lectures
   (b) a test hearing
   (c) listeners, or official examiners
   (d) having to do with hearing
   (e) those present at a performance

(*Answers on p. 173*)

ROOT—CAP, CAPT, CIP, CEPT

1. The___(a)___herded their___(b)___into a prison.
For many years later, they would___(c)___their
listeners with tales of their adventures during the
___(d)___.
   (a) seizers
   (b) those who were seized
   (c) hold spellbound
   (d) the act or event of seizing

(Answers on p. 174)

ROOT—CED, CESS

1. After both sides felt that no more___(a)___could be
made, the South threatened to___(b)___from the
Union. Even in the face of___(c)___, Lincoln refused to___(d)___to Southern demands, and the
Civil War began, to last for more than five years until
the guns finally___(e)___firing at Appomattox.
   (a) yieldings   (c) withdrawal   (e) stopped
   (b) withdraw   (d) yield

(Answers on p. 174)

ROOT—LEG, LECT

1. Before one can___(a)___a proper course of action,
he must first___(b)___all available data.
2. The___(c)___proceeded to the___(d)___to inform
the audience of some of the trickier___(e)___aspects
of the case that would soon come before the courts.
   (a) choose
   (b) gather
   (c) speaker (originally a reader)
   (d) a stand from which one reads or speaks
   (e) having to do with law

(Answers on p. 174)

ROOT—MITT, MISS

1. The messenger___(a)___great confidence as he handed the___(b)___to his commander, completing his___(c)___. Then he used the radio___(d)___to inform GHQ that the task was completed. He was sure he would earn a___(e)___for his valiant service.

   (a) sent forth, radiated
   (b) message, letter, something to be delivered
   (c) task, errand
   (d) that which sends, sends across
   (e) a formal warrant or authorization, granting certain powers

(Answers on p. 174)

ROOT—PELL, PULS

1. Some said the President acted on___(a)___, when he used the powers granted under the___(b)___draft laws to send American troops to___(c)___Communist invaders in Asia. Ten huge___(d)___-driven planes carried the men.

   (a) a spontaneous inclination
   (b) obligatory, enforced
   (c) to drive back
   (d) instrument that provides power to drive

(Answers on p. 174)

ROOT—ROGA

1. The more closely the hero was___(a)___, the more ___(b)___his exploits seemed.

   (a) questioned
   (b) performed to a greater extent than required

(Answers on p. 174)

ROOT—SENS, SENT

1. The___(a)___of Joyce's prose is remarkable.
2. Humans are___(b)___beings, as distinguished from plants.
3. The senator's speeches, though always___(c)___, usually lacked common___(d)___.

   (a) accuracy of perception
   (b) capable of physical feeling
   (c) terse and pithy, sometimes pompously formal
   (d) perception, judgment, intelligence

(Answers on p. 174)

ROOT—VID, VIS

1. Despite the acuteness of the pilot's___(a)___, the ground was still___(b)___to him, because the fog had cut___(c)___to practically zero. However, by listening to ground communications, he could easily ___(d)___the situation.

   (a) sight
   (b) unable to be seen
   (c) degree of clearness in atmosphere
   (d) to form a mental image of

(Answers on p. 174)

PREFIX—A, AB, ABS

1. Appalled by their king's___(a)___, the populace forced him to___(b)___, after___(c)___forever his right to the throne.

   (a) deviations from rectitude or propriety
   (b) to formally relinquish a high office
   (c) repudiating an oath or a right

(Answers on p. 174)

PREFIX—A, AD

1. The senator made the accusation that spies had been
   ___(a)___given___(b)___to secret files which
   would greatly___(c)___the cause of the enemy. He
   demanded that they be___(d)___immediately.
   - (a) heedlessly
   - (b) the means of approach
   - (c) move forward
   - (d) seized

(*Answers on p. 174*)

PREFIX—ANTE

1. As the guests waited in the___(a)___of the beautiful
   southern mansion, they could not help thinking of the
   magnificence of___(b)___plantation life.
   - (a) a room before or leading into a chief room
   - (b) before the Civil War

(*Answers on p. 174*)

PREFIX—BEN, BENE

1. The bishop beamed___(a)___at his___(b)___, as
   they knelt for his___(c)___.
   - (a) with good will
   - (b) those who confer benefits
   - (c) blessing

(*Answers on p. 174*)

PREFIX—CO, COM, CON

1. Before the assembly___(a)___, the delegates met sep-
   arately and___(b)___about the possibility of interna-
   tional___(c)___for an all-out well-___(d)___at-
   tempt to defeat cancer.
   - (a) gathered together, came to order
   - (b) exchanged ideas
   - (c) collective action
   - (d) harmoniously functioning

(*Answers on p. 174*)

PREFIX—DE

1. ____(a)____as opposed to induction means to proceed from general principles to particular facts.
2. Some attribute the____(b)____of the great monarchies to the personal____(c)____of the monarchs.
3. The____(d)____farmland looked like a giant____(e)____.
   - (a) a method of reasoning
   - (b) wane
   - (c) deterioration
   - (d) stripped bare
   - (e) profanity

(*Answers on p. 174*)

PREFIX—DI, DIF, DIS

1. After a long, ____(a)____address by the chairman, a motion was made to____(b)____the previously announced aims of the committee. A____(c)____followed, and the____(d)____of opinion was so fundamental, that finally the committee was____(e)____.
   - (a) roving from one subject to another
   - (b) repudiate
   - (c) altercation, argument
   - (d) unlikenesses
   - (e) dissolved

(*Answers on p. 175*)

PREFIX—E, EX

1. Disorderly persons will be____(a)____.
2. The price was____(b)____.
3. Every rule, no matter how____(c)____, has its ____(d)____.
   - (a) thrown out
   - (b) unusually high
   - (c) rigorous, precise
   - (d) exclusions

(*Answers on p. 175*)

153

PREFIX—IN, IM, (INTO)

1. The speech____(a)____that it was illogical to ____(b)____the rise in____(c)____to the lowered tariff. The speaker was effective, and by his logic____(d)____ many of his listeners to change their views.
   (a) suggested
   (b) charge, credit
   (c) goods coming into a country
   (d) penetrating
   (e) prevailed upon by persuasion

(*Answers on p. 175*)

PREFIX—IN (NOT)

1. The____(a)____of the foreman and the____(b)____of his orders were____(c)____.
   (a) lack of skill
   (b) state of being difficult to understand
   (c) unexplainable

(*Answers on p. 175*)

PREFIX—OB

1. His quick action, despite the____(a)____of his superiors, ____(b)____the need for further meetings. He didn't allow the____(c)____of others to____(d)____ his plans.
   (a) stubbornness
   (b) anticipated, thereby making unnecessary
   (c) lack of sensitivity or perception
   (d) impede, block

(*Answers on p. 175*)

PREFIX—PER

1. The odor of the nearby factories____(a)____the air. It seemed it would last____(b)____, it____(c)____every part of the houses and shops in the area.
   (a) diffused or spread throughout

    (b) enduringly

    (c) diffusing or spreading throughout (different word from *a*)

(*Answers on p. 175*)

PREFIX—SYN, SYL, SYM

1. There are almost no exact____(a)____in the English language.
2. The____(b)____was called to attempt a____(c)____of the findings of the last year's research.
       (a) words which have the same, or nearly the same, meaning
       (b) a conference; a collection of opinions
       (c) combination of parts into a whole

(*Answers on p. 175*)

SUFFIX—AGE

1. The celebrity took____(a)____at the unflattering story.
2. Washing clothes in cool water will prevent____(b)____.
3. The breakdown meant a complete____(c)____of work.
       (a) offense
       (b) growing smaller
       (c) ceasing

(*Answers on p. 176*)

SUFFIX—ESCE, ESCENT, ESCENCE

1. After a long harangue, all the members____(a)____to the demands.
2. ____(b)____is measured in lumens.
3. Some say____(c)____is the best time of life.
       (a) submitted
       (b) amount of light
       (c) period between childhood and adulthood

(*Answers on p. 176*)

SUFFIX—FIC, FY

1. Sociologists are increasingly aware that America is a highly____(a)____society.
2. ____(b)____should be used with care.
3. The original theory was greatly____(c)____by subsequent research.

    (a) made in layers
    (b) sleeping pills; drugs that induce sleep
    (c) made broader or bigger

(*Answers on p. 176*)

SUFFIX—ISM

1. ____(a)____is a perpetual enemy of science.
2. ____(b)____was a natural reaction to the rather dour classical art that immediately preceded it.
3. ____(c)____long threatened to gain a permanent foothold in modern Europe.

    (a) positiveness of opinion, usually unwarranted positiveness.
    (b) state of being romantic, anticlassical
    (c) political theory based on state supremacy

(*Answers on p. 176*)

Now that you have completed these exercises, don't feel that you are finished with vocabulary improvement. A good vocabulary takes a lifetime to develop and can only be acquired by generating a real interest in words that you read or hear. When you encounter a new word, try to determine its meaning, then check it in a dictionary. Notice how it is used; notice its various shades of meaning. A good vocabulary is such an essential tool for reading, writing, and speaking, that it will be to your great advantage to continue to improve it.

Day X

Skipping and Skimming Exercise #6

Question: Why do scientists discount the processes by which various smaller particles are annihilated as an example of a complete release of energy?

Since $E=mc^2$ (energy equals the mass times the speed of light squared), scientists are able to calculate energy release by simply calculating the reduction in the size of the mass of the releasing atom or particle. In other words, the amount of possible energy is always equal to the amount of the present mass. In that case, shouldn't it be true that we would be able to produce vast amounts of energy by completely annihilating the mass of particles? Any particles left intact would represent energy untapped. Perhaps it should be, but scientists say we will never be able to completely annihilate matter so as to obtain the maximum energy output. It is true that some smaller particles, such as the meson, have been annihilated, but the process has always involved an "unnatural" particle, or one that was first created, and the energy release was never greater than the energy that went into creating the particle in the first place.

Eye-Swing Exercise #7

His spirits seem to have been much depressed. "I too am wretched," he wrote to his friend Bryan, in the course of the winter. He says that he meditated resigning his seat and going to Europe. He seems to have been suffering under a complication of trials, the mystery of which his biographers had best not attempt to penetrate; for his wails of despair, sometimes genuine, but oftener the effect of an uncontrolled temperament, tell nothing more than that he was morbid and nervous. "My character, like many other sublunary things, hath lately undergone an almost total revolution." No such change is apparent, but possibly he was really suffering under some mental distress. There is talk even of a love affair, but it is very certain that no affair of the heart had at any time a serious influence over his life.*

This is what you should have circled:
      spirits   depressed.
   wretched,"
      winter.   meditated resigning   seat
                                                          suffering
                     trials,   mystery
biographers   not   penetrate;
         despair, sometimes genuine,   oftener
         uncontrolled temperament,
               morbid   nervous.   character,
                                             undergone
            revolution." No   change   apparent,
possibly   suffering   mental distress.   talk   love affair,   certain   no affair   heart   serious
influence

*Henry Adams, *op. cit.*, p. 44

Circle the emotionally charged or loaded words or phrases in the following selections. Are there any fallacies in the reasoning of either?

A—

Yes, I'm against censorship, not only of books, but in any form whatsoever. Once we start to censor—once the judges get their claws into one more of our freedoms, it's just a little step further to censor speech and just one more little step or a whole series of little steps until we find ourselves right in the middle of a police state. This country was founded on the right of every man to be *free*. And we're losing our freedoms every day. I ask you, how can we ever hope to defeat Russia if we keep doing our best to imitate her?

B—

Say what you like about constitutional rights. The Constitution never gave anybody the right to spread *filth*. If we ever lose out to Communism, it will be because the whole moral fiber of our nation has been steadily rotting away. The slime they sell on the newsstands today is an insult to any parent who's trying to give his kids a decent Christian upbringing. I think we have a perfect right to censor dirty books, or anything else as rotten—that's the only way we'll ever be sure of staying free.
(*Answers on p. 176*)

Timed Reading Exercise #4

Pre-read and read the following selection. Try to do it faster than the last one. When you finish, divide the number of minutes it took you into 1,300 words to obtain your words per minute score, then answer the questions on the selection.

In view of the description given, may one be gay upon the Encantadas? Yes: that is, find one the gaiety, and he will be gay. And indeed, sackcloth and ashes as they are, the isles are not perhaps unmitigated gloom. For while no spectator can deny their claims to a most solemn and superstitious consideration, no more than my firmest resolutions can decline to behold the spectre-tortoise when emerging from its shadowy recess; yet even the tortoise, dark and melancholy as it is upon the back, still possesses a bright side; its calapee or breast-plate being sometimes of a faint yellowish or golden tinge. Moreover, every one knows that tortoises as well as turtles are of such a make, that if you but put them on their backs you thereby expose their bright sides without the possibility of their recovering themselves, and turning into view the other. But after you have done this, and because you have done this, you should not swear that the tortoise has no dark side. Enjoy the bright, keep it turned up perpetually if you can, but be honest and don't deny the black. Neither should he who cannot turn the tortoise from its natural position so as to hide the darker and expose his livelier aspect, like a great October pumpkin in the sun, for that cause declare the creature to be one total inky blot. The tortoise is both black and bright. But let us to particulars.

Some months before my first stepping ashore upon the group, my ship was cruising in its close vicinity. One noon we found ourselves off the South Head of Albemarle, and not very far from the land. Partly by way of freak, and partly by way of spying out so strange a country, a boat's crew was sent ashore, with orders to see all they could, and besides, bring back whatever tortoises they could conveniently transport. It was after sunset when the adventurers returned. I looked down over the ship's high side as if looking down over the curb of a well, and dimly saw the damp boat deep in the sea with some unwonted weight. Ropes were dropped over, and presently three huge antediluvian-looking tortoises, after much straining, were landed on deck. They seemed hardly of the seed of earth. We had been abroad upon the waters for five long months, a period amply sufficient to make all things of the land wear a fabulous hue to the dreamy mind. Had three Spanish custom-house officers boarded us then, it is not unlikely that I should have curiously stared at them, felt of them, and stroked them much as savages observe civilized guests. But instead of three custom-house officers, behold these really wondrous tortoises —none of your schoolboy mud-turtles—but black as widower's weeds, heavy as chests of plate, with vast shells medallioned and orbed like shields, and dented and blistered like shields that have breasted a battle—shaggy too, here and there, with dark green moss, and slimy with the spray of the sea. These mystic creatures, suddenly translated by night from unutterable solitudes to our peopled deck, affected me in a manner not easy to unfold. They seemed newly crawled forth from beneath the foundations of the world. Yea, they seemed the identical tortoises whereon the Hindoo plants this total sphere. With a lantern I inspected them more closely. Such worshipful venerableness of aspect! Such furry greenness mantling the rude peelings and healing the fissures of their shattered shells. I no more saw three tortoises. They expanded—became transfigured. I seemed to see three Roman Coliseums in magnificent decay.

Ye oldest inhabitants of this or any other isle, said I, pray give me the freedom of your three-walled towns.

The great feeling inspired by these creatures was that of age:—dateless, indefinite endurance. And, in fact, that any other creature can live and breathe as long as the tortoise of the Encantadas, I will not readily believe. Not to hint of their known capacity of sustaining life, while going without food for an entire year, consider that impregnable armour of their living mail. What other bodily being possesses such a citadel wherein to resist the assaults of Time?

As, lantern in hand, I scraped among the moss and beheld the ancient scars of bruises, received in many a sullen fall among the marly mountains of the isle—scars strangely widened, swollen, half obliterate, and yet distorted like those sometimes found in the bark of very hoary trees—I seemed an antiquary of a geologist, studying the bird tracks and ciphers upon the exhumed slates trod by incredible creatures whose very ghosts are now defunct.

As I lay in my hammock that night, overhead I heard the slow, weary draggings of the three ponderous strangers along the encumbered deck. Their stupidity or their resolution was so great that they never went aside for any impediment. One ceased his movements altogether just before the midwatch. At sunrise I found him butted like a battering-ram against the immovable foot of the foremast, and still striving, tooth and nail, to force the impossible passage. That these tortoises are the victims of a penal, or malignant, or perhaps a downright diabolical enchanter, seems in nothing more likely than in that strange infatuation of hopeless toil which so often possesses them. I have known them in their journeyings to ram themselves heroically against rocks and long abide there, nudging, wriggling, wedging, in order to displace them, and so hold on their inflexible path. Their crowning curse is their drudging impulse to straightforwardness in a belittered world. Meeting with no such hindrance as their companion did, the other tortoises merely fell foul of small stumbling blocks; buckets, blocks, and coils of rigging; and at times in the act of crawling over them would slip with an astounding rattle to the deck. Listening to these draggings and concussions, I thought me of the haunt from which they came; an isle full of metallic ravines and gulches, sunk bottomlessly into the hearts of splintered mountains, and covered for many miles with inextricable thickets. I then pictured these three straightforward monsters, century after century, writhing through the shades, grim as blacksmiths; crawling so slowly and ponderously, that not only did toadstools and all fungous things grow beneath their feet, but a sooty moss sprouted upon their backs. With them I often lost myself in volcanic mazes; brushed away endless boughs of rotting thickets; till finally in a dream I found myself sitting cross-legged upon the foremost, a Brahmin similarly mounted upon either side, forming a tripod of foreheads which upheld the universal cope.

Such was the wild nightmare begot by my first impression of the Encantadas tortoise. But next evening, strange to say, I sat down with my shipmates and made a merry repast from tortoise steaks and tortoise stews; and supper over, out knife, and helped convert the three mighty concave shells into three fanciful soup-tureens, and polished the three flat yellowish calapees into three gorgeous salvers.*

1. Gaiety is
   a. possible on the Encantadas.
   b. not possible on the Encantadas.
   c. possible on the Encantadas if the person likes turtles.
   d. not considered on the Encantadas.
2. The author views turtles as
   a. pleasant little animals.
   b. symbols of the two-sidedness of a situation.
   c. frightening spirits.
   d. none of the above.

*The Shorter Novels of Herman Melville, op. cit., pp. 153-6

3. When one of the islands was sighted
   a. the crew refused to go near it at first.
   b. the crew was frightened.
   c. the crew was curious.
   d. its name was Albemarle.
4. The boat crew was ordered to
   a. scout for inhabitants.
   b. find fresh water.
   c. look around the island.
   d. collect coral.
5. The boat's crew brought back
   a. three tortoises.
   b. two tortoises.
   c. brightly colored coral.
   d. custom-house officers.
6. The ship had been at sea
   a. three months.
   b. four months.
   c. five months.
   d. six months.
7. The tortoises
   a. looked like mud turtles.
   b. had heavy dark medallions.
   c. had heavy black shells.
   d. made strange croaking noises.
8. The tortoises inspired the author with a feeling of their
   a. great weight.
   b. unfortunate existence.
   c. pretty shells.
   d. great age.
9. The tortoises possessed
   a. great endurance.
   b. strange powers.
   c. valuable shells.
   d. small battering rams.

10. The tortoises were used for
   a. souvenirs.
   b. food.
   c. transportation.
   d. trophies.

(Answers on p. 176)

Vocabulary Study #4

Following is a list of the more unusual words from the selection you have just finished reading. You will need a dictionary to complete this exercise.

unwonted—not accustomed; uncommon; unusual. Anglo-Saxon *un* (not) and *wunian* (to dwell).

> Don't confuse "wont" with "wanton." What do they mean?

antediluvian—of the time before the Flood, hence very old; ancient. L. *ante* (before) and *diluvium* (flood).

> What is the meaning of each of the following words? Be sure and check them in your dictionary.
> ante bellum   antecedent   antedate
> What does the abbreviation "A.M." mean?
> Do not confuse the prefix "ante" with the prefix "anti." What does "anti" mean?

orbed—shaped like an orb; spherical or global.

impregnable—not capable of being captured or entered by force; unshakable; unyielding; firm. L. *im* (not) and *prehendere* (to take).

The words "impregnate" and "impregnable" are almost opposite in meaning. Even though they look alike, they have different prefixes. What is the difference?

citadel—a fortress; stronghold; refuge. Italian *cittadella* (little city).

obliterate—to blot out; erase. L. *ob* (against) and *litera* (letter).

The prefix "ob" can connote: to; toward; opposed to; upon; over; completely; totally; inversely. What is its meaning in each of the following words?

obdurate	obfuscate	oblate
obese	objurgate	oblivious
object	oblique	obscenity
obligation	obnoxious	obscure
obloquy	obeisance	
obedient	obituary	

antiquary—a person who studies antiquities. L. *antiquus* (ancient, old).

What is the difference between:

old
antiquated
ancient
archaic
antique
obsolete

cipher—(noun) 1. zero. 2. nonentity. 3. code or secret writing. 4. the key to a code. 5. an intricate weaving together of letters; a monogram. 6. any Arabic numeral. —(verb) 1. to solve by arithmetic. 2. to write in code.

exhume—to dig out of the earth; disinter. L. *ex* (out) and *humus* (ground).

Define the following words. Be sure and check them in your dictionary.

excerpt	excommunicate	execrable
excogitate	exculpate	exigency
excrescence	exegesis	expatiate
executor	exorcize	expire
exonerate	expedite	extemporize
expectorate	expurgate	extradite
expropriate	extort	extricate
extirpate	exclave	
excise	excoriate	

defunct—no longer living; extinct. L. *de* (from, off) and *fungi* (to perform).

The prefixes of the following words have different meanings. What are they?

detrain	decline	defrost	denigrate

infatuation—the state of being infatuated; a foolish or unreasoning attraction or passion. L. *in* (intensifier) and *fatuus* (foolish).

Would only a fatuous person believe in an *ignis fatuus?*

inextricable—see "extricate" under "exhume" above.

concave—hollow and curved like a section from the inside of a sphere. L. *con* (intensifier) and *carus* (hollow).

salvers—trays on which letters, cards, refreshments, etc., are placed for presentation. L. *salvare* (to save).

In ancient times, it was customary for a servant of a king to taste food to protect the king from poisoning: hence the word "salver."

Read Twice as Much

You have come to the end. Let us review the techniques we have discussed. First of all, you became a *phrase reader;* that is, you began to take bigger and bigger bites out of the page with each eye stop. You did this by changing the focus of your eyes, by not looking directly into the print, but slightly above it; in other words, you are a *space reader*. Then, rather than wasting your eye span in margins, you began to *indent* on each line; you made your first and last eye stops on a line slightly in from the margin, so you, in effect, saw nothing but print. To become a more efficient phrase reader, you practiced recognition of word groups, *logical* word groups. As the final step in your physical approach to the page, you became a *sight reader*. You practiced the *mumbling* technique to eradicate the habit of saying or hearing each word that you read.

In order to improve your comprehension as you read faster, you began to *pre-read*. Now you pre-read short articles by reading their introduction and conclusion, and the key words from the sentences of each paragraph. Books are pre-read by using all the appended aids the publisher furnishes—the introduction, table of contents, index, appendix, etc. Another fast comprehension device was *key-word reading,* and in order to develop this ability, you practiced recognizing the key words in the selections. When you are reading to answer a question now, you *skip and skim,* and save all the time normally spent on irrelevant material. To develop your concentration and your comprehension even further, you became an active, *questioning* reader, trying to *anticipate* what the author would say, trying to discover his conclusions beforehand. And this naturally led you to be a *critical reader*—always on the lookout for loaded words or fallacious arguments.

Then, to refine your reading skills, we discussed various ways to get the most out of different materials. You have a separate way of reading newspapers, magazines, non-fiction books and novels. You know how to handle book reviews, business letters, and business publications. And last but not least, you have improved your vocabulary. You have become familiar with word roots and word origins, and you have had to use your dictionary.

You have come to the end. But just to the end of the book, not to the end of reading or practice. The skills you have learned are not quite *habits* yet. They will be—but you'll have to do your part. Be *conscious* of what you're doing every time you read. Think of the skills you should apply to everything you encounter. Then apply them. In a short while, you won't have to think about them any more. They will come naturally—but only if you continue practicing.

One more suggestion. Don't use your new skills to read what you always read but in half the time. Use them to read *twice as much* as you ever read before.

Answers

Answers to sample sentence completion exercise (p. 33)

Importance	Many
Summarizes	Much
Never	

Answers to sample paragraph development exercise (p. 34)

4, 3, 1, 5, 2

Answers to sentence completion exercise #1—A (p. 42)

Promise	Venture
Ahead	Old
Opportunities	Casualties
New	
(or Equivalents)	

Answers to sentence completion exercise #1—B (p. 42)

Observant	Rise
Rewards	Fall
Rise	Characteristic
Favor	Reflection
Depressed	
(or Equivalents)	

Answers to paragraph development exercise #1—A (p. 49)

3, 6, 1, 4, 2, 5

Answers to paragraph development exercise #1—B (p. 50)

5, 1, 4, 7, 2, 8, 6, 3

Answers to questions on page 65

1) B	3) A	5) D	7) D	9) B
2) B	4) C	6) D	8) C	10) D

Answers to sentence correction exercise #1 (p. 76)

1. *extraordinary*—replace with ordinary
2. *endearing*—replace with annoying
3. *destructible*—replace with indestructible
4. *implausible*—replace with plausible
5. *imprecision*—replace with precision

Answers to critical reading exercise #1 (p. 78)

dragged . . . socialism

everybody pay for . . . some collect on

stretch tentacles

private life

principles on which great country was founded

welfare state

opening of West

railroads

War for Independence

individual initiative

erosion of power . . . increase of welfarism *(no logical basis for causal relationship between these assumptions, which are not even backed up by proof)*

Answers to timed reading exercise #1 (p. 82)

1) D	3) B	5) D	7) C	9) C
2) C	4) D	6) D	8) D	10) C

Answers to paragraph development exercise #2—A (p. 89)

3, 2, 4, 1

Answers to paragraph development exercise #2—B (p. 90)

3, 1, 5, 4, 2

Answers to sentence correction exercise #2 (p. 90)

1. *raised*—replace by lowered
2. *efficiency*—replace with inefficiency
3. *less*—replace with more
4. *cynic*—replace with idealist
5. *unsuccessful*—replace with successful

Answers to sentence correction exercise #3 (p. 95)

1. *obscure*—replace with discover
2. *antitoxins*—replace with toxins
3. *like*—replace with different from
4. *flexible*—replace with inflexible
5. *dropping*—replace with rising

Answers to timed reading exercise #2 (p. 101)

1) A	3) B	5) B	7) D	9) C
2) D	4) B	6) B	8) B	10) D

Answers to critical reading exercise #2 (p. 108)

A. This is called the "argument from illegitimate authority." Weakness lies in trying to claim that "everybody knows" or "everybody does," etc. This assumption is patently untrue.

B. The statement implies that John Doe's pitching prowess also makes him an authority on hair tonic.

Answers to sentence completion exercise #2—A (p. 110)
sell, hold, outside, extra, regular, paid, investment, emergencies, ready, reserve, investments (or equivalents).

Answers to sentence completion exercise #2—B (p. 110)
clear, wealthy, rich, market, small, feeling, persuasive, untrue (or equivalents).

Answers to critical reading exercise #3 (p. 116)

1. Compare the statement to:

> All dogs have four legs.
> My cat has four legs.
> Therefore, my cat is a dog.

2. Weakness lies in the conception of a complex world in terms of an "either . . . or" choice. Also, argument by analogy (black, gray, white) is always weak.

Answers to timed reading exercise #3 (p. 133)

1) B	3) D	5) A	7) A	9) D
2) C	4) B	6) B	8) A	10) A

Answers to critical reading exercise #4 (p. 143)
worming its way
egghead professors
teacher factories
strangle hold
bloodthirsty hordes of pimpled sadists
throwback to cave-man

good old three R's
$20,000-a-year eggheads . . . ivory towers
respect for home, family, religion, country
switchblade

This is an example of "after this, therefore because of this" reasoning. The author gives no reason for his opinion that progressive education has led to rising juvenile crime rates. He just assumes that it has. The term "progressive education" itself has taken on its own emotional coloring and should have been clearly defined before the author went any further.

Answers to paragraph development exercise #3—A (p. 143)

    3, 5, 1, 4, 2

Answers to paragraph development exercise #3—B (p. 144)

    4, 7, 5, 1, 3, 6, 2

Answers to sentence correction exercise #4 (p. 144)

1. *disprove*—replace with prove
2. *little*—replace with great
3. *highly*—replace with hardly
4. *retained*—replace with dropped
5. *improper*—replace with proper

Answers to vocabulary exercises (p. 148)

AG, ACTUS:

    a) actually
    b) actuate
    c) actuality
    d) actuarial
    e) active

AUD, AUDIT: (p. 148)

    a) auditorium
    b) audition
    c) auditors
    d) auditory
    e) audience

CAP, CAPT, CIP, CEPT: (p. 149)

- a) captors
- b) captives
- c) captivate
- d) capture

CED, CESS: (p. 149)

- a) concessions
- b) secede
- c) secession
- d) cede e) ceased

LEG, LECT: (p.149)

- a) select
- b) collect
- c) lecturer
- d) lectern
- e) legal

MITT, MISS: (p. 150)

- a) emitted
- b) missive
- c) mission
- d) transmitter
- e) commission

PELL, PULS: (p. 150)

- a) impulse
- b) compulsory
- c) repel
- d) propeller

ROGA: (p. 150)

- a) interrogated
- b) supererogatory

SENS, SENT: (p. 151)

- a) sensitivity
- b) sentient
- c) sententious
- d) sense

VID, VIS: (p. 151)

- a) vision
- b) invisible
- c) visibility
- d) visualize

A, AB, ABS: (p. 151)

- a) aberrations
- b) abdicate
- c) abjuring

A, AD: (p. 152)

- a) inadvertently (note double prefix)
- b) access, admittance, admission
- c) advance
- d) arrested, apprehended

ANTE: (p. 152)

- a) antechamber
- b) ante-bellum

BEN, BENE: (p. 152)

- a) benevolently
- b) benefactors
- c) benediction

CO, COM, CON: (p. 152)

- a) convened
- b) conversed
- c) co-operation
- d) co-ordinated

DE: (p. 153)

- a) deduction
- b) decline
- c) decadence
- d) denuded
- e) desecration

DI, DIF, DIS: (p. 153)
- a) discursive
- b) disavow
- c) disagreement
- d) difference
- e) disbanded

E, EX: (p. 153)
- a) ejected
- b) exorbitant
- c) exact
- d) exceptions

IN, IM, INTO: (p. 154)
- a) implied
- b) impute
- c) imports
- d) incisive
- e) induced

IN (NOT): (p. 154)
- a) incompetency
- b) inexplicitness
- c) inexplicable

OB: (p. 154)
- a) obstinacy
- b) obviated
- c) obtuseness
- d) obstruct

PER: (p. 154)
- a) permeated, pervaded
- b) permanently
- c) pervaded, permanently

SYN, SYL, SYM: (p. 155)
- a) synonyms
- b) symposium
- c) synthesis

AGE: (p. 155)
    a) umbrage
    b) shrinkage
    c) stoppage

ESCE, ESCENT, ESCENCE: (p. 155)
    a) acquiesced
    b) luminescence
    c) adolescence

FIC, FY: (p. 156)
    a) stratified
    b) soporifics
    c) amplified

ISM: (p. 156)
    a) dogmatism
    b) romanticism
    c) Fascism

Answers to critical reading exercise #5 (p. 159)

A.—get claws . . . freedoms   B.—filth

police state
founding of country
defeat Russia

lose out to Communism
moral fiber rotting
slime
Christian upbringing
dirty books
rotten

The biggest sin that both of the selections committed is known as *ignoratio elenchi* or missing the argument. The point in question was obviously whether the government could or could not censor books. But both parties persisted in arguing about Communist domination, police states, parental problems, etc., and never sought to find out just what rights the government has or does not have to censor books. Arguments of this nature serve to do nothing but let off excess steam.

Answers to timed reading exercise #4 (p. 163)

1) A	3) D	5) A	7) C	9) A
2) B	4) C	6) C	8) D	10) B